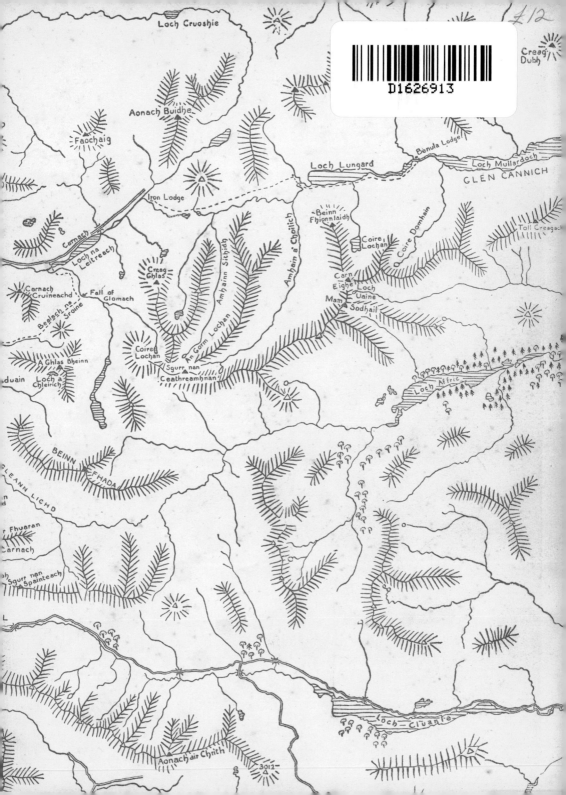

Stewart Coronie,
67 Lakenheath,
Southgate,
London, N. 14.

KINTAIL SCRAPBOOK

KINTAIL SCRAPBOOK

BY

BRENDA G. MACROW

WITH
PHOTOGRAPHS BY

ROBERT M. ADAM

OLIVER AND BOYD
EDINBURGH: TWEEDDALE COURT
LONDON: 98 GREAT RUSSELL STREET, W.C

1948

FIRST PUBLISHED 1948

THIS BOOK IS SET IN 12 POINT GARAMOND

PRINTED IN GREAT BRITAIN
BY ROBERT CUNNINGHAM AND SONS LTD., ALVA
FOR OLIVER AND BOYD LTD., EDINBURGH

TO MY MOTHER AND FATHER

PREFACE

I HAVE no excuses to offer for this book. It was just one of those things I had to do. My sole justification for writing it is that I, too, have loved Kintail—have lived (for too brief a space, alas!) among her hills and glens, soaking myself in her history and folklore, making it as nearly as possible my own.

My reasons for so doing are many, and difficult to explain. Perhaps it may suffice to say that I was one of those who, falling once under the spell of this wild corner of the Western Highlands, vowed then and there to return, and stay, and give some articulate voice to those half-glimpsed glories which had set their seal upon my eyes and heart. I can but trust that the quality of the material may compensate for the faultiness of execution.

So here it is—the record of a summer in Kintail, among friends whose hospitality and many kindnesses to the " stranger at the gates " will remain ever a delightful memory. That the record is incomplete, I am only too well aware. Yet, I have hopes that it may serve, in some measure, to reflect the enchantment of this still-to-be discovered land—its moods and its magic—its undertone of changeless beauty— its reassurance of the peace that awaits the war-weary among the " untrodden ways."

My sincere thanks are due to my friends in Kintail, Glen Shiel and Lochalsh, without whose assistance and advice this book could never have been written.

BRENDA G. MACROW

CONTENTS

CONTENTS

ILLUSTRATIONS

CHAPTER I

WE TAKE THE PLUNGE

I LEFT London on a night of blue twilight and faint, drizzling rain. I had packed up sandwiches to eat on the train, but thought it prudent to go out and have dinner before starting. My sister and I found a little Hungarian place where we had wiener schnitzel and salad, with some rather sickly trifle to follow. While we were eating, my little Skye terrier, Jeannie, lay under the table, registering strong disapproval.

Poor Jeannie! No doubt she was thinking of the comfortable cottage we had lately left, and wondering into what discomforts and difficulties this latest wild jaunt of her mad mistress was going to land her.

Jeannie hates travelling. She makes no pretence of liking it. Some strange phobia about trains has caused her, ever since puppyhood, to break out in a cold sweat at the mere rattle of wheels over sleepers, the distant " chuff-chuff " of a sleepy engine. Nothing I can do or say will console her. Euston Station is her idea of hell; and I knew that even the dose of bromide I had brought for her in my handbag would do little towards making her relax on this, the first really long train-journey of her life. She would just lie rigid all night beside me in the " sleeper," looking at me miserably from under her long fringe of grey hair, wondering what she had done to deserve such prolonged torment. And it was impossible for me to explain to *her* the reason for this sudden upheaval following a wild orgy of packing—this long run to the North which would seem to her to be going on for ever.

I

It was even difficult for me to explain it to myself. I only knew that there was a place in Scotland which was calling me back, and that I could no longer resist the call. Gradually, in a thousand little ways, this place had of late been intruding itself upon my notice, cunningly weaving its spell from afar, until I had become obsessed with a hunger for the bens and glens of the Highlands—an all-absorbing desire to renew contact with that corner of the West Coast which would ever be to me the Lost Land of Eternal Youth.

And so—I was going back to Kintail. And, already, sitting in the train at Euston, I could feel the cool mountain wind blowing off the snowfields—smell the sharp tang of peat—hear the soft footsteps of Spring rustling over heathery braes. And, suddenly, I was quietly confident that I was doing the right thing, and that Jeannie and I would find a long-sought happiness among the hills where I, a " Sassenach " by birth, had left my heart.

The train started with a long hiss and clatter of wheels. The lights of Euston went slowly past the window, then faster and faster, until they blended into one long line of wavering gold. Then—darkness, save for the errant glimmer of a window in the shadowy buildings on either side of the line. We were away!

I had only one companion in my compartment, a young woman who told me her destination was Inverness. We took a lower berth each, and, for a while, chatted about a variety of current topics, while the wheels beneath us fell into the rhythm of a fast-cantering horse. Jeannie, as I had anticipated, buried her head in the crook of my arm and refused to be comforted.

Soon, the warmth of the carriage and the monotonous sing-song of the wheels began to take effect. I took out the bottle of bromide and poured half of it down Jeannie's throat, taking the other half myself. Then we lay down and put out the light.

It seemed to me that years passed—slow, drowsy, lazy years of warmth and slumber. Yet, I was not really asleep, and all the time I was conscious of Jeannie's rigid, shaggy little body under the blanket beside me. I don't think she closed her eyes. After what seemed an eternity wherein I lay making up songs and stringing verses together in time to the rhythm of the wheels, there was a jolt, and a voice shouted " Perth! " with that unmistakable Northern intonation which I had come to love and remember. I looked at the luminous face of my watch, spoke to Jeannie, and pulled the blanket up from the floor. The light went on, and a young man entered. We exchanged a brief greeting before, as quietly as possible, he climbed up into the berth above my neighbour. Jeannie did not even growl. The song of the wheels started again, and I knew no more.

When I awoke, it was light, and there was a young woman in the berth above me, though I did not remember her coming in. By and by, the four of us rubbed the sleep from our eyes and started up a conversation. Sandwiches came out, though a dining-car had been put on at Perth. Later, we went in relays to breakfast, and had porridge and finnan haddie. Indeed, I thought, we had left the South and its customs far behind.

Northward, northward, we sped through the brightening morning. Over the unforgettable Pass of Killiecrankie; between dark folds of pine-forest, as yet unawakened by the caress of Spring; across brown moorland where a few stray sea-gulls fluttered like scraps of paper over a mass of tumbled hills. We crossed granite bridges where, far below, a brown burn sped on its headlong way over white stones, catching the fitful rays of the sunlight and holding them captive for a moment in shallow pools before it overflowed and burst into whirls of silver foam. Past Dalwhinnie, Kingussie, and Aviemore, where the great white crests of the Cairngorms leaned against a cold blue sky. Then, almost too soon, we were tumbling out on to the platform at Inverness and counting our odd pieces of luggage as they were transported over to the branch line for the West Coast.

How describe the remainder of that journey, which is well known to every lover of the Western Isles? The thousand-and-one halts; the unfolding tapestry of the unchanging hills; the names that are like a melody once heard and never forgotten. Dingwall, Achanalt, Achnasheen, Achnashellach and, at last, Plockton, where you begin collecting the baggage again for Kyle of Lochalsh.

It was raining when we arrived—but Jeannie, at least, did not care. She was too happy to be out of the train. The poor little creature had refused all meat and drink for nearly eighteen hours, and I lost no time in finding her some clean water, which she drank daintily and without haste. We then set about finding accommodation for the night.

We crossed the ferry to Kyleakin and tried first at a farm in Skye, but without success. It was raining hard, and Jeannie was not at all impressed by the land of her ancestors. Returning to the mainland, a fellow-passenger from the " Misty Isle " remarked on her breed, which he said was known nowadays as the " Show Skye," the " Working Skye " being a much smaller dog, possibly through being crossed with the Cairn terrier. Jeannie was no more impressed by this discussion of her ancestry than she had been by the rugged island for which I had expected her to feel at least a tinge of pride. By this time, she was too wet to care about anything, and I was fast reaching the same state. Without further dallying, therefore, we hastened to the Nor-West Hotel, where we were welcomed, wet as we were, with open arms. I decided to take Jeannie back to Skye on a day better suited to the revelation of its undoubted charms.

I hardly remember sleeping better than I did that night. An excellent dinner and a hot bath had induced the sort of deep, dreamless slumber that I have always coveted but seldom achieved. If I were conscious of anything at all, it was of a strange happiness, a sense of contented expectation. The long journey was nearly over. To-morrow we would be in Kintail!

We drove from Kyle of Lochalsh to Dornie in the brilliant sunlight of the April afternoon. The 'bus, we were told, had met with an accident the week before; but it had been arranged for a shooting-brake from the Loch Duich Hotel to take its place. It was a quiet drive, although the brake was full. Jeannie, who is not nervous of cars, sat contentedly on my lap, looking out of the window.

As we swung out of Kyle and began to climb the first steep curve of the coast road, the lovely panorama of the isles was spread out before us, offering us a glimpse of unchanging beauty. There were Pabay, Longay, Scalpay, the beginning of Raasay—and there, beyond, lay the great, snow-streaked, cloud-haunted company of the Cuillin, calm and at peace in the warm Spring air. Anew, I thrilled to their strange, soul-shaking mystery—anew, I climbed in spirit the huge round hump of Marsco, the black knife-edge of Blaven, the great, jagged cliffs of Sgùrr Alasdair with faint ribbons of cloud swirling around his knees.

Then, all too soon, the road swung inland, mounting through scarred grey and brown moorland on to the rise overlooking Balmacara.

From here, other (and even dearer) hills came into view—the Five Sisters of Kintail, crowned with snow and resting their heads against the soft pillows of the cloud. That first glimpse of them as they rose, pale and serene, beyond the shining curve of Lochalsh, was like meeting old friends and finding that the passage of time was a dream . . .

The road ran on, and the hills were lost behind the nearer slopes of forest and dead brown heather. Only the sharp point of Beinn na Caillich, across Lochalsh, seemed determined to follow us to our destination.

We reached Dornie at tea-time. It was quiet, peaceful and friendly, just as I had remembered. The restored fortress of Eilean Donan stood proud and aloof upon its island, touched by the long shadows which crept across Loch Duich from the hills above Letterfearn. The little rows of grey houses, clustered along the water's edge, winked the blind eyes of their windows in the golden light of the afternoon. The toll-bridge had mellowed since my last visit, and no longer looked out of place in these tranquil surroundings.

B

I stopped to exchange a greeting with the lady at the toll-house, who welcomed me with true Highland courtesy and charm. Then I gathered up my belongings and set about finding temporary lodgings until I should discover a small furnished house. I found excellent accommodation at the first place I tried—the Dornie Hotel—whose staff at once provided me with a welcome tea. Afterwards, in the bedroom, I opened a tin of stewed steak for Jeannie, and she ate the lot, with every sign of approval. She seemed to realise that, for the time being, we were home!

After a short rest, we went out for a walk, to renew our acquaintance with the Kintail countryside. The hill-road mounted swiftly up the brown brae. Already, the wayside was starred with a riot of Spring flowers—pale-faced primroses, tossing daffodils and windflowers fluttering their snowy skirts around the feet of the tall pines. We tramped on to the summit of the rise, and there sat down on a rough grey wall, looking out across the quiet mirror of Loch Duich far below. To our right, the fast-sinking sun traced a pathway of shattered gold across the wide curve of Lochalsh, and beyond this the Cuillin rose mistily against the western sky. Loch Duich was dark and still, streaked by the darker shadows of its hills and trees. Along the far shore, the wooded hills above Letterfearn ran down towards the Màm Rattachan road and the deep blue hollow of lovely Glen Shiel. At the head of the loch, the Five Sisters were gathered close together in the dusk like blue-robed nuns, each with a white coif around her brow. There was no sound but the quavering bleat of new-born lambs and the soft crackle of little wild things among the dry heather.

It was a strange, cool evening of lights and shadows—and a fitting return to the hills of my heart. . .

Those first days in Kintail seemed to fly past on dizzy, golden wings, like a summer butterfly. Jeannie and I made one or two walks over the hills, to test our capabilities and familiarise ourselves with the ground over which we would be stravaiging during the months ahead. The weather, apart from a stray shower, held good—surprisingly so for the West Coast at this time of the year.

Most of our first fortnight, however, was spent in a frenzied search for a house. The position, we soon discovered, was akin to that in the South—or, to put it bluntly, there was nothing to be had! One or two sumptuously-furnished residences were available, it is true, but these were either too large or two expensive for our limited means, and we were obliged to thank them politely and pass on.

One day, I found a little granite house along the Kintail side of Loch Duich, and, to my delight, discovered that it was empty. Further investigation, however, proved it to be in such a state of dilapidation that it was being used as a byre. We decided that it might be possible to do a little better than that, and continued our search.

And then, quite suddenly, in the middle of our third week in Dornie, we found it! A shepherd's bothy on a little rise overlooking Nostie, with two good front rooms, a kitchen and water laid on indoors! We were told that it had been empty for about eighteen months, being in need of repair—but we *might* get it as temporary accommodation if we went and saw the landlord personally.

I set out at once, found Mr. Matheson ploughing a field, and the deal was done in a matter of ten minutes. We could have the cottage, he said, for two months anyway. After that, it might be wanted for a shepherd; but at least such an arrangement would give us time to look for something else.

In transports of delight, we went to examine our new residence. It was built of the usual grey stone, with walls about two feet thick and a large red corrugated-iron byre attached. Looking across from the front door, we could see Lochalsh flashing in the sunlight and the grey roofs of Nostie and Avernish nestling among budding larch-trees. Smoke was drifting up from their chimneys and floating away like a blue film on the quiet evening air. We had a stretch of " lawn " in front of the house, bounded by a little wall in whose cracks and crannies the shy ferns were uncurling to the light. There were two gnarled apple-trees, some rose-bushes, a lilac-bush and one or two stray pheasant-eye narcissi, already on the verge of opening. There were also several sheep with their lambs, which excited Jeannie's immediate disapproval. With a little cunning stalking, however, we succeeded in getting them through the gate and out on to the hill.

Standing at the front door—or, better still, beside the little grey wall—we looked down a mile-long stretch of smooth road, at the end of which the clustered hills of Kintail, fold upon blue fold, offered peace to the unquiet heart. We looked into the deep blue valley of the Glennan, banked on one side by the steep cliffs beyond Bundalloch and on the other by massive, sprawling Beinn a' Mheadhoin, over whose broad shoulder we could glimpse the proud head of Sgùman Cóinntich, one of the mighty guardians of Killilan. One of the nearer peaks still bore traces of unmelted snow, and this I identified with binoculars as Boc Mór, the Big Roebuck, which I had hopes of climbing as soon as time permitted. I stood for a long time watching the patterns of the shadows deepen and change over these unchanging hills—and I knew that if I could not write in this lovely, quiet place, then I should hide my head for shame and try no more.

After a while, Jeannie and I went into the cottage. The two front rooms were, as we had been told, in very good condition apart from the fireplaces. These we mended with pieces of iron off the salvage-heap. Our living-room had dark polished wood walls and a wooden floor, while in the other room, our bedroom, the walls were papered and the floor of concrete. There was a splendid sink in the big kitchen—but no sanitation of any description! However we were accustomed to life in the country, and had already made plans about such trivialities as that.

The greatest difficulty of all, of course, was that we had not so

OLD HOUSES AT DORNIE

much as a stick of furniture. The next item on the agenda was, therefore, an immediate trip to Kyle of Lochalsh. Meantime, we should continue to live in luxury at the hotel, enjoying civilisation while we might.

We took the " bus " to Kyle the next day, and spent an amusing, if somewhat exhausting, morning in the furniture-shop. Fortune was definitely on our side, for buying furniture in these days is no easy business! We succeeded in getting a dining-table, (synthetic refectory, but quite charming), a kitchen-table, a large and well-sprung sofa, a padded ottoman, a mattress, two Army blankets, a broom, one sauce-pan, a frying-pan and various oddments of second-hand crockery. We also bought a large oil-painting of the Highlands by Wellwood Rattray (irresistible, this! I can live without knives and forks, but never without books and pictures). We had no bed, no curtains, no chairs, nothing to cook on, nothing to wash in, no kettle, no pillow and no cutlery of any kind except a boy-scout knife! However, Jeannie agreed that we would manage somehow.

We arranged for the furniture to be delivered, bade farewell to the charming lady who had borne with us for so long, and went to lunch with our new friend Mrs. Adams at the Nor-West Hotel. Then we returned to Dornie, walked up to the cottage, and set some violets and primroses in rusty salmon-tins off the salvage-heap to give it a festive air. I had mentally arranged the furniture and hung up the picture, and, already, it looked like home.

On the Monday, our goods and chattels were delivered, and we moved in. To test my repairs to the fireplaces, I lighted three fires. All of them promptly went out. I foraged around for more pieces of iron and arranged a damper in the one in the living-room, which smoked. Finally, I had at least one fire burning brightly. Fortunately, Mrs. Fraser at the furniture-shop had included a Valor heater with my belongings, so I put a saucepan of water on it and made some tea. Jeannie and I then sat down on the sofa and shared a biscuit.

A little later, my landlord, Mr. Matheson, came up to mend the gate so that we would no longer be troubled by the inquisitive sheep. He also put up my picture, which was too heavy for me to lift. We admired it together, noting how the light from the window gave it life and colour. Already, I knew the Mathesons were my friends.

In the afternoon, I wrote to the South for some curtains, plus a carpet and a bed which I happened to have in store. I also wrote to a hardware shop for a Primus stove and one of those admirable contrivances which advertises itself boldly as an " Elsan Chemical Closet."

I opened a tin of fish for supper, and Jeannie condescended to share it, with a comment to the effect that she would have much preferred raw lights. Then we went round and locked all the doors, filled a hot-water bottle, and returned to the living-room with a tray for the morning.

And so to bed, for our first sleep in our new home, with the fire burning merrily and the little room full of the tang of pine-smoke. Outside, the hill-wind was howling on a long, eerie note—but Jeannie and I had not a care in the world. We turned out the lamp (borrowed), nestled into the deep and well-sprung sofa, and pulled the Army blankets over the two of us. I buried my head in a (borrowed) pillow, and Jeannie edged herself into the curve of my knees. The blankets tickled at first, but soon the warmth began to take effect, and drowsiness stole over us both.

Outside, no doubt, the quiet hills were watching us, wondering if we were mad or just moonstruck.

Inside, the firelight flickered on the polished wood walls, the array of friendly books on the mantlepiece, our " Wellwood Rattray " in its heavy gilt frame.

" Jeannie," I said, sleepily, " this is it. This is our new home."

A heavy snore was the only response.

Presently, I, too, slept. . .

CHAPTER II

LOCH LONG AND KILLILAN

WE had arranged about the rations and the meat. We had seen the baker and the coalman. Everything, we discovered, would be delivered to the door. The only thing we would have to collect would be our mail, from Miss Graham at the post-office, and our milk from Mathesons' farm.

All that was lacking was a front-door key, this having been mislaid by the previous tenant. After spending several days climbing in and out of the bedroom window, I went to Kyle and bought a padlock, which was efficient if not too ornamental.

Every day, the hills put on new garments, as if for our especial delight. There was more snow on the high peaks, and at times I would have given the world for a box of paints. Returning one evening from the farm, I was brought to a dead halt by the view along Loch Duich. How shall I describe it? The loch was like a sheet of steel, over which the light played and flickered, streaking it here with pure silver, there with dull metallic grey. Green grass ran down to a weed-entangled shore along which the white houses—one with an emerald-coloured roof—seemed to reflect the pale rays of the fading sun. On the Letterfearn side, the slopes of the hills were patched with the fresh green of budding larches, interspersed with the purple of shadowy pines. The castle, flooded with sunlight, was a quiet golden-grey, with no shadow or darker colour but the deeper grey of the roof. At the head of the loch, the high hills were pure silver where the sun played over their frozen faces. Towards Glen Shiel and the

Saddle, the silver merged softly to pale mauve and then to purple as the slopes ran down beyond the reach of the sun.

I could have stayed there forever, watching the light change and change again across those snow-clad fastnesses until they faded into the mist. If I could only paint. . . But what painter in the world (with the possible exception of Finlay MacKinnon, who knew and loved these hills as his own), could have caught that magic hour of light and shadow, and made it live ?

On another evening, we sat in the garden at Nostie, and saw the hills in a different mood. Just before dusk, they all flamed suddenly blood-red, with deep wine-coloured shadows—all except the one nearest to us across Lochalsh, which remained an odd yellowish green. The effect was weird in the extreme. We could not see the sun, which was setting away beyond the ragged Cuillin; but the nearby hills were all on fire with its light. The sky above remained a cold, transparent blue, without even a hint of gold. It was as if the hills were exuding fire from within, radiating heat from the glowing core of the Earth.

If I had tried to paint *that* scene, I should have been accused of Surrealism. People would have said it was too strange to be believed— forgetting that the greatest Surrealist of all is often Mother Nature herself.

Towards the end of my first week at the cottage, the Primus and Elsan arrived, to be followed by the bed and carpet. The last-named was especially welcome. Bare boards are apt to put splinters in the feet, if not watched. And I can never be bothered to look for my slippers in that first drowsy ten minutes when I get up to make tea.

A day or so later, a parcel arrived containing two tea-cloths, a dish-cloth and some provisions. We were now in the height of civilisation. One of the tea-cloths was much too good to wipe dishes on, being pure linen with a green border. It was soon doing proud duty as our first table-cloth, and even lent an air of dignity to the " tea-tray " which, disguise it how we would, remained uncompromisingly the lid of a corn-bin!

12

The mattress we had purchased in Kyle exactly fitted the newly-arrived bedstead. We arranged the pillow and blankets, registered approval—then took them all off again and went back to the sofa. (Did I mention previously that the bedroom had a concrete floor?) Besides, it was still cold at nights, and we enjoyed going to sleep in the fitful glow of a log-fire.

The sea-air was making me sleep as I had never slept in my life. Often, I would wake to find sunshine pouring in through my improvised curtain (a silk scarf held up by safety-pins!). Outside, the fields would be suffused with new gold, the flowering whins waving softly in the wind. Sometimes, a black-and-white collie was racing up and down across the blown grass and bog-cotton, full of the joy of living. Stretched out flat in a mad gallop, with his bushy tail sleeked by the wind, he could have been taken for a fox except for his colour. He made me envious, and Jeannie and I were soon up and out in the sunshine.

Often, we would emerge from the cottage into a world of shimmering gold, with huge, fluffy clouds clotted over the eastern hills. I would lie flat on the dry grass, reading or writing, while the sun poured down upon me, burning my body through my clothes. More often than not, I would have my meals outside on a tray.

They were lazy days, these. Only Nature, it seemed, carried on with her ceaseless task of recreating beauty. The gean-trees flowered, and the blossoms fell in a white shower on to the warm grass. The ash-buds, like little clusters of black grapes, etched fantastic patterns against the sky, before bursting into a cloud of yellow foam. Gull and curlew cried lornly over the brown folds of the heather—and I was prey to a secret longing, a nostalgia for things I could not name. Perhaps it was not a real longing at all—just one of those queer figments of the imagination that come with the Spring.

They began to burn the heather on the hills, and the smoke of it gave the curious effect of ground-mist rising into a clear sky.

Sometimes, it seemed not to be moving at all, just hanging in white, fluffy columns, as if the stationary clouds had dropped feelers down to the earth. Then, when the wind rose, it would be driven in thick clouds down the rusty slopes, rolling almost into the glens before it faded and was lost on the boisterous air.

At evening, the homing birds flew slowly across a quiet sky, their wings beating in time to some sweet, sad rhythm of earth and sea. The yellow-green larches moved sensuously in the wind. Across the road, beyond the greystone wall of my garden, the long, dry, cream-coloured reeds would tap out a message on the evening air. The smoke would die on the hills—the hills themselves fade from brown to grey, from grey to a chaste, distant blue. Somewhere, a cuckoo would call ecstatically, its clear note echoing among the grooves and precipices of this lovely, heaped-up land. The sun would die, and the earth become a pale, demure maiden, half-veiling herself behind the blown gossamer of blue mist.

I would gather my papers together and go in, leaving Jeannie to play contentedly with an old shoe in the grass. Jeannie is the Peter Pan of all dogs—though, if she were human, she would now be roughly the same age as myself.

There came a day when there was hardly a breath of wind. We sat out in the sun, letting the drowsy warmth sink into our bones. Every sound came, sharp and distinct, across the golden air, even the " chip-chop " of a spade where a woman was digging in a neigh-bouring field. Before that, she had been spreading manure. I felt lazy, lying in the sunlight only half-using my brains, when there were people around me working like that. Now she was standing up, leaning on her spade, surveying the admirable results of her toil. Behind her, the low hills sloped gently down to the blue expanse of Loch Alsh—but she looked only at the warm brown earth. . .

The unsteady bleat of young lambs mingled with the Spring-song of the birds. A bee flashed across my eyes on some urgent errand, like a motor-cyclist rushing for the doctor, or speeding for the sheer love of speed. Across the road, a white cockerel led his harem with short, jerky movements over a ploughed field.

The yellow shooting-brake came up the long, straight road, going into Kyle. The sun glistened on its polished woodwork and chromium fittings. A sparrow was twittering on the top of my chimney. Two butterflies—fritillaries of some kind—disported themselves over the whispering grass. There was a faint blue haze over the hills.

"Jeannie," I said, putting away my papers, "This is too good a day to waste. We're going out!"

And I went indoors to pack up sandwiches.

We walked slowly along the Killilan road in the blazing sunshine, having not yet decided where to go. The bluebells were out in the woods, and the silver birches at last awakening from their long sleep. Primroses still starred the banks in a profusion of scattered gold. Dog-violets opened their blue eyes among the moss and dead pine-needles.

The road was gravel, white and hot in the sun. For a long time, knobbly Beinn a' Mheadhoin dominated the entire landscape, shutting out the sky. At his feet, across the shining mirror of Loch Long, the little cottages of Bundalloch clustered together along a shore dark with drying seaweed.

We trudged past the narrow neck of the loch, climbed a rise, and found ourselves looking down into Sallachy, with mighty Ben Killilan and the more jagged outline of Sgùman Cóinntich beyond, like two giants guarding the green sweep of forests below.

The tide was out at the head of Loch Long, and sea-birds were swooping over the tangle of black weed—mallard, heavy-winged heron, curlew, black-backed and black-headed gull, oyster-catcher, red-shank and the inevitable "hoodies," wheeling and diving in swift arcs of coloured light, their strange, lonely cries echoing across the still air.

I fell to wondering about the loch, and the traditions that surround it. Loch Long—said to be named after the long boat, or galley, in which St. Fillan was brought back from Iona to his last resting-place at the head of the loch, thereafter called Killilan. One version of the story has it that this St. Fillan was the son of a chieftain of Kintail, converted to Christianity by the teachings of St. Columba. He went to Iona to visit his leader, and while there, he died. His body was laid in a galley and brought back up Loch Alsh to the land of his birth. The boat anchored for a while at a spot at the mouth of Loch Long, which is still called " Camas Longart "—the Bay of the Long Boat. This galley, it is said, was the longest ever seen on the loch. The boat finally beached at the head of the loch, where St. Fillan's remains were carried ashore and buried at what is now Killilan, where there is also a well named after the saint. According to tradition, he sleeps under a sod brought from Iona.

There is another story about St. Fillan which has connections with Loch Long. When the Saint was travelling in France, he always carried a hazel-staff from Kintail. One day, he met an alchemist who remarked on the staff and asked him if he would go back and get the white serpent which had its hole under the root of the tree on which the staff had grown. This was said to be at the north-east end of Loch Long. St. Fillan went back, kindled a fire, and put a pail of honey near the spot. Presently, out came the serpent, and crawled into the pail. St. Fillan had to cross seven streams with the pail before he was safe from the other serpents following their captured king. The Elchaig was one of these. He rested on a hill called The Hill of Tears and composed a poem before proceeding on his way. When he arrived in France, the alchemist put the pail on a fire to boil, and told the Saint on no account to touch any bubbles which might rise to the surface. Unthinkingly, St. Fillan burst the first bubble, put his scalded finger in his mouth, and was thereafter possessed of magical powers of healing. He then returned to Kintail, where he became

renowned as the greatest physician of all time. (This story seems to be a variation of the Icelandic saga of Sigurd the Volsung and the Dragon's Heart.)

It has never been finally established whether these two tales refer to the famous St. Fillan (who, incidentally, was not a contemporary of St. Columba), or to another ecclesiastic of the same name. Certainly, this St. Fillan is famous enough in Kintail.

Among other celebrated heroes said to be buried at Killilan is Fionnla Dubh nam Fiadh—Black Finlay of the Deer—who had a hand in starting the great feud between the men of Kintail and the Macdonalds of Glengarry. Black Finlay was a forester of Glen Cannich who encountered a Macdonald hunting deer on his territory, having taken refuge there after committing some crime. High words passed between them, and Finlay shot the trespasser and cast his body into a lochan. Shortly afterwards, twelve Glengarry men, out for revenge, called at Finlay's home without realising where they were, and his wife invited them in and poisoned them. All died but one. This one went back to Glengarry, collected eleven more men, and returned for vengeance. On the way, they met Finlay himself, cutting wood, but did not recognise him, as they were strangers. He sent them on to the house, slipped round to a back window, and asked his wife to hand out his bow and arrows. He then got up a tree, called out in a loud voice, and shot the men one by one as they came out of the house! Finally, this intrepid warrior came to a sad end when a Glengarry leech, having been told who he was, killed him in the course of " treatment " for a wound in the head.

Meditating on these old stories, I had wandered far into the misty realms of legend, and my pace had slowed down accordingly. The sun poured down on us out of a hard blue sky. Jeannie's tongue was

LOCH LONG AND DORNIE VILLAGE (*Before Bridge was Built*).

hanging out, and I would have given anything for a glass of lemonade. (I daren't start on the peat-brown water of the wayside streams. I get such a taste for it that I never know when to stop!). Jeannie, however, plunged into a sunlit burn and drank to her heart's content.

A little further along the road, I found the answer to my own prayer—a little " road-house " run by two charming ladies, where I found not only cooling drink, but refreshing talk.

I had now made up my mind where we were going. Emerging from this heaven-sent establishment in the back of beyond, we crossed the white bridge over the River Ling and followed a rough cart-track down to the smooth waters of the Elchaig. There were some pure-bred Highland cattle grazing along the shore—vast golden beasts with deep chests and great, curving horns. Their tiny calves were curled up like balls of ginger wool among the long grass at their feet.

There was no bridge over the Elchaig at this point, and I had to ford it on foot. It was wide, shallow and very stony. Part of the time Jeannie was almost swimming, but she stuck gamely to her guns and made the opposite bank with considerably less difficulty than myself. A shower of silver drops fell on to the grass as she shook the gleaming waters of the Elchaig from her shaggy coat.

We ate a belated lunch under a budding rowan-tree, while the Highland cattle came down to drink on the far side of the stream. Knee-deep, they stood cooling themselves on the fringe of the current, their wise faces and huge spreading horns somehow giving the impression of great age. Their slow, ponderous movements were eminently suited to the quiet beauty of the scene.

After a short rest, I put on my thick socks and boots, and we rambled on to Camas Linne, a cluster of little grey houses at the foot of brown braes. From here, we struck up the rough hillside towards the lacy waterfall. Below us, the ground rolled away and down to where the great sweep of Glen Elchaig carved a green gash in the hills, with the river curving in a wide " S " between smooth fields.

We could see the high hills overshadowing Loch na Leitreach—Faochag, Aonach Buidhe—but most dominant of all was the nearer hump of Càrnan Cruineachd, thrusting up his massive chin at the sky.

We climbed on, but soon stopped again, this time to look at the fall. It was a thin, delicate veil of blue, floating down the opposite hillside over black rocks that shone in the sun. Lower down, it disappeared between softly-waving larches into a dark hole leading, one supposed, to some faery cavern under the earth.

It was hard to leave it, but we climbed on. At last, we topped the rise and struggled over increasingly rough ground on the track that runs round behind wild Beinn a' Mheadhoin and so down to Bundalloch.

We found the source of the River Glennan, a mere trickle among yellow sphagnum and black peat. Lower down, we could see the whole course of the stream winding between scarred grey hills back to Loch Long. Time after time, we lost the track among scree and boulders. Ahead, the loch gleamed silver, luring us on. Away on the skyline, the massive company of the Cuillin loomed dimly blue through gathering mist. The roughness and moisture of the ground combined to make our progress extremely slow.

We reached Bundalloch at sunset—and the longest part of the whole journey seemed to be that three mile tramp back to Nostie, where the little cottage stood waiting for us in the dusk.

CHAPTER III

A VISIT TO THE CASTLE

THE rain came down the hills in a cloud of moving silver. For the moment, at least, the long dry spell was interrupted by more typical West Coast weather. Over Loch Alsh, the heavy grey clouds unfolded their smoky banners, shutting out the sun.

It was definitely not the right day for a long excursion " on the hill." So, after breakfast, I took my courage in both hands and requested permission to look over Eilean Donan Castle. It was readily granted, and I was soon trudging along the rain-spattered lane towards the restored stronghold of Kintail, grey and aloof upon its island.

As I crossed the bridge I could not help thinking that, from an aesthetic as well as strategic point of view, the position could hardly have been bettered. On every hand (even in the rain) the eye is captivated by scenery that defies description. The grey length of Loch Duich, sweeping down to the blue-robed Sisters of Kintail. The wooded slopes of Totaig with their pine and larch-trees nodding like green plumes in the wind. Loch Alsh, and the black-headed gulls dipping over white-crested waves. Dornie Bridge, and the blue curve of water towards Loch Long, with scattered white houses hugging the lonely shore.

Then, the Castle itself, blown into ruins in 1719 by Government forces under Captain Boyle—and restored between 1912 and 1932, under the orders of Lt.-Col. John MacRae-Gilstrap, by Farquhar MacRae of Auchtertyre, who died six months before it was opened. The architect who designed the present fortress was Mr. George

Mackie Watson, and the work is said to have been carried out with only local labour and materials. Much of the stone used has yet to be " weathered "; but from the mainland Eilean Donan presents a picture of quiet grandeur which blends well with its surroundings.

Like most of the old fortresses, it is haunted by the grey ghosts of history and legend. Originally, the Castle was a vitrified fort. Part of this masonry is still to be seen, having the appearance of scorched rock; but the secret of its building has been lost.

At one time the Castle was said to have consisted of seven towers, and, according to the " old tales," was built by a Matheson who understood the language of the birds. This young man obtained his strange gift by receiving his first drink as a baby from the skull of a raven. He became a great linguist, and achieved much renown among his people. For many years, he travelled abroad, and when he returned, he was entertained by his own father, who did not recognise him, thus fulfilling a prophecy of the birds.

His learning soon brought him into favour with Alexander II, who commissioned him to build Eilean Donan Castle as a stronghold of defence against the Danes and Norsemen. This was in the early part of the thirteenth century—the precise date of the building of the Castle is not known.

One of the first Constables of the Castle was a certain Kenneth Matheson. He was succeeded by the Irishman, Colin Fitzgerald, who received the appointment as a reward for his services at the Battle of Largs, that great conflict, in 1263, between Alexander III and Haco of the Norsemen. Colin Fitzgerald married Kenneth Matheson's daughter, and their son, called Kenneth after his grandfather, was the founder of the great Clan MacKenzie.

The name Eilean Donan, (of which there are a variety of spellings), is thought to mean " Donan's Island," and to have associations with St. Donan, a follower of St. Columba, who founded a monastery on the Isle of Eigg. In April of the year 617, Eigg was invaded by

C

Pictish pirates, and this Saint, together with his little community of about fifty converts, was slain.

His precise connection with Kintail is not very clear, but like St. Duthac and St. Oran (whose name, according to some, lives on as that of the highest peak of the Five Sisters), St. Donan is a familiar figure in the old legends of the district.

But there is also another—and very charming—story of how Eilean Donan got its name; and I am assured that this is one of the old tales which has not previously appeared in print. From as far back as the days of the old sagas, there has been a colony of otters around this little island; and it is well-known among the Celtic people that the otter tribe (" Cù donn," or " brown dog " in the Gaelic) have a King. This King is a lovely, lissome creature with a coat of silver or pure white. The story woven around Eilean Donan tells how once a King of the Otters died, and his robe of silver was buried on the little island in Loch Duich, under the foundation-stone of the original Castle— hence " Donan," which may have been derived from " donn " (brown). I confess that this story appeals to me even more than the one about the saint—perhaps because it reveals something of the essentially romantic and imaginative character of the ancient Gael . . . and, for that matter, of his twentieth-century descendant, though many a modern Highlander will assure you that the " old knowledge " has vanished into the limbo of things forgotten.

I stopped outside the portcullis of the Castle, looking up at the old stones and thinking how many strange and terrible things they must have witnessed. Many of these same stones must have seen Randolph, Earl of Moray, come sailing up Loch Alsh in 1331, on a visit to the Castle in his capacity as Warden of Scotland. Perhaps, at that time, some of these great blocks had formed part of the walls on which the heads of fifty slain " misdoers " were exposed in honour of his arrival. Justice was stern in those days, and Randolph himself is said to have remarked that the sight of those heads was sweeter to him than any garland of roses!

In 1537, in the heyday of the old Clan Feuds, Donald Gorm Macdonald of Sleat attempted to take the Castle from the Lords of Kintail, having heard that it was very poorly garrisoned. The rumour which had reached his ears was, indeed, true, for the only men in Eilean Donan at that time were the Constable, John Dubh Matheson, and the watchman! However, a certain Duncan Macgillechriosd, a redoubtable warrior of the district, heard of Donald Gorm's approach and hurried to the Castle. There, he barred the door and took up his stand with the defenders. Presently, the Macdonald galleys came sailing up the loch, and soon the assailants were battering on the Castle gate. This, however, resisted all their efforts, so they began shooting arrows through the narrow slits which served as windows. One of these arrows killed the Constable; and thereafter Duncan and the watchman were in what might be known to-day as a " tight corner." They did not despair, however, and presently Donald Gorm himself came ashore and began walking round the fortress, looking for the best place from which to launch an assault. With his last arrow, through a hole which is still to be seen in the old wall of the Castle, Duncan took careful aim, and hit Macdonald in the foot. In pulling out the barb, the chieftain of Sleat severed the main artery. Nothing his men could do would stop the bleeding, and at last he was conveyed to a little island opposite Ardintoul, thereafter named Làrach Thig Mhic Dòmhnuil, where he died. After this, the Macdonalds seem to have abandoned their project for the time being, though it is recorded that they attempted to set fire to the Castle, destroyed some boats, and succeeded in doing a certain amount of damage. The tragedy of their leader's death, however, had somewhat damped their ardour, and presently they re-embarked in their birlinns and sailed away.

Thereafter, Duncan Macgillechriosd applied to the Lord of Kintail for the Constableship of Eilean Donan—thinking, no doubt, that he had more than earned the honour. His application, however, was refused, and the only material reward he seems to have obtained was

John Dubh Matheson's widow in marriage! Greatly disappointed, he left Kintail and lived for some years on the Lordship of Lovat—though he eventually returned to end his days at Inverinate, on the shore of Loch Duich. On the family tree of the Clan MacRae in the restored Castle, he appears as "Temporary Constable"—so, after all, he came near to achieving his heart's desire!

There is another old story regarding the Castle, set in the previous century. In the year 1452, the Countess of Ross fell deeply in love with Alexander, Lord of Kintail, and sent for him to come to her Court. Finding that he did not love her, she imprisoned him. By sending his gold ring to Eilean Donan, she succeeded in enticing the Constable, a Macauley, out of the fortress. He, too, was imprisoned, and her men took possession of the historic stronghold of Kintail. Meantime, however, a party of Mackenzies had waylaid some of the Countess's followers and dressed themselves in their prisoners' tartan. Thus disguised, they gained admission to Eilean Donan and seized the new Governor and all his men, refusing to release them until the Countess had freed the Lord of Kintail and his Constable.

During the troubled times of the Stuarts, Eilean Donan came frequently into prominence. In 1650, after the execution of Charles I, it was garrisoned by the Scottish Parliament, with the intention of overawing the people, who were almost wholly in sympathy with the Stuart cause. This garrison treated the people very roughly, and insisted that the Castle should be provided with fuel for the winter. One day, they sent a party of soldiers to Inverinate to enforce their demands, under the command of a certain John Campbell and his sergeant, Blythman. The Kintail men, led by Donald Òg MacRae, rebelled, killed Blythman and Campbell among others, and put the rest of the garrison to flight. "Campbell's Croft" and "Blythman's Ford" were named in memory of this episode. The garrison shortly afterwards left, being in fear from that time of the men of Kintail. In 1653, the Castle was garrisoned by Cromwell.

During the Rising of 1715, Eilean Donan was taken by Government troops, but was recaptured by the men of Kintail just before the Battle of Sherriffmuir. They engineered this by asking the Governor of the Castle if he would send some troops to help take in the harvest. He agreed, and sent most of the garrison—with unfortunate results for himself!

Before the Battle of Sherriffmuir, tradition says that the Stuart supporters had a dance on the Castle roof—a light-hearted prelude to the tragedy of the battle itself, when many Kintail men were killed, being in the second line of Mar's army. It is said that Sherriffmuir made fifty-eight widows in Kintail alone—a large number in the " barbarous " days before the invention of the dive-bomber.

In the abortive rising of 1719, a fierce battle took place in Glen Shiel, at the head of Loch Duich. The Highlanders were assisted by Spanish troops under the Duke of Ormonde's Expedition, sent by Cardinal Alberoni—but here, again, the men of Kintail lost heavily. This battle and its subsequent developments marked the end of Eilean Donan as an ancient fort, for it was blown into ruins by a ship of war under Captain Boyle " so that traitors might have one haunt the less in which to plot mischief against the king and the laws."

And here is an eye-witness account of the Castle as a ruin, written in 1890 by John Sinclair, from whose book, *Scenes and Stories of the North of Scotland* (lent to me by my helpful " landlady,") the above quotation is taken. This was over a century after the destruction of the Castle, when the kind hands of time had added beauty to the shattered shell of the once-proud fortress of Kintail:

Close by the entrance of Loch Duich, on the Dornie side, lies the low rocky islet which is crowned by the picturesque ruins of Eilandonan Castle. Seen from the water, they appear to stand just above the beach, but looked at from the shore itself, they stand out, lofty and grim, against the hills of Skye. The main portion of the building was a square keep eighty feet high, with various courts, wings and archways on either hand. On the sloping bank nearest to the shore of the mainland, a well of clear-springing water was shielded by masonry, and high walls flanked the path between it and the keep. As at present seen, the walls are shattered and crumbling away; the turrets show many a gap and rent which the friendly ivy tries in vain to hide; the lintels and archways are broken and jagged; yet if human words and deeds were stored up in the stones which first rang with them, what romances and tragedies lie around us and at our very feet! . .

And, even to-day, the atmosphere of romance and tragedy lingers. Who shall say that the famous men of Eilean Donan are dead? There are strange things in the hills, and it may yet be that when the wind is high and the sea beating against the rocks, the old Clan Chiefs still carry on their ancient feuds around the ghost of the historic stronghold. Here, perhaps, in some unchanging spirit-world outside the reach of time, is Kenneth MacKenzie, fifteenth-century chief of Kintail, sending his unfortunate one-eyed wife back to her father, John of Islay, mounted on a one-eyed horse, attended by a one-eyed servant and followed by a one-eyed dog!* Here, at the Battle of Park (which was the result of the above episode), is the same Kenneth, assisted by his brother, Hector Roy, and the redoubtable Donnacha Mór na Tuagh, or Big Duncan of the Battle-Axe, who refused to take part in the fight until he had had what he considered to be sufficient recognition from his Chief—and then did such colossal damage with his battle-axe that the fray resulted in an overwhelming victory for the men of Kintail. Here, out of all this, is the growing feud between the Chief's brother, Hector Roy, and the MacKenzie's illegitimate son by the second lady of his choice, Agnes Fraser of Lovat. Though this " marriage " was afterwards declared legal by the Pope, Hector Roy refused to recognise the child, John of Killin, as the heir to the Kintail estates, and seized them for himself. John, however, proved more than a match for his uncle when he attained manhood, and finally beseiged Eilean Donan Castle and captured Hector Roy at Fairburn, after which his claim to the Chieftainship of Kintail suffered no further opposition.

Here, again, setting out in the soft light of a moonlit evening, is

* This story is also told in connection with Donald Gorm MacDonald and the daughter of the celebrated " Rory Mór " of the Isles.

the grey galley of Duncan MacRae, grandson of the Duncan Macgillechriosd who killed Donald Gorm of Sleat. From the tower of the Castle, the Laird's wife watches anxiously, her gay plaid perhaps floating out on the light sea-breeze. Her husband, the MacKenzie, is away in Mull, and she has just heard that the Glengarry birlinns are heading back towards Loch Alsh, after their raid on Loch Carron. We can imagine Duncan reassuring her as he steps down into the boat which is to intercept Angus Òg Macdonald, under cover of the night, on his way through Kylerhea. Now the men have cast off, and the slim birlinn is drifting away up Loch Alsh, the voices of its crew wafting back across the water as it disappears into the pearly haze of the gathering dusk. How anxiously Lady MacKenzie waits in the tower, while the night-hours drag by on soft, silent feet and the grey owls hoot over the dark slopes of the close-gathered hills. At last— the distant, muffled splash of oars. Cheery voices lilting over the Gaelic, and the dim shape of a boat—one boat—looming through the morning mist. Lady Mackenzie strains her eyes through the uncertain light of early morning—then runs down the stair to meet the boat as it grates on the shore below. Yes! It is her own galley, with Duncan smiling and waving in the bow, and every man in his place at the oars. Enraptured, she learns that the Glengarry men suffered a heavy defeat, having run on to the Cailleach Rock in the half-light and put themselves completely at the mercy of the men of Kintail. There, in the bottom of the boat, lies the body of their leader, Angus Òg, and the only injury among Duncan's men is a cut hand, inflicted by accident by the victim himself. Lady MacKenzie at once gives orders that the funeral of the Glengarry chieftain shall be properly attended to, and on the following day, so tradition has it, he is buried " in a manner suitable to his rank " at Kilduich, in the same grave as some of Lady MacKenzie's own children.* Thus, in an age of blood and murder, we find the

* I am greatly indebted to the Rev. Macauley of the Manse, Inverinate, for lending me a copy of the Rev. Alexander MacRae's *History of the Clan MacRae* (privately printed), from which many of these old stories are taken.—B.G.M.

strange touches of chivalry so lacking in the more " civilised " warfare of to-day.

I think the modern Eilean Donan, with its central heating and comfortable furnishings, would have overawed me had it not been for the kindly caretaker. But, with Miss Macaulay, everything fell into an ordered pattern. Here was the " Billet Room " (now a sitting-room, with Persian rugs covering the flagstones). This was the MacRae and MacKenzie crest, and this the striking oil-painting of the Highland ball before the Battle of Sherriffmuir. Through here was the banqueting-hall, and the wee gallery where the piper played while the chieftains feasted. At one end of this imposing room was an illuminated family tree of the Clan MacRae, brought to life by apt and intriguing comments written beside the names. Here was the aforementioned Duncan MacGillechriosd, " temporary Constable of Eilean Donan," who killed Donald Gorm of Sleat. Here was Farquhar, from whom was descended that branch of the Clan known as the " Black MacRas "—and here another " MacRa " who was noted for the magnificent funeral given to him on his decease! Almost opposite were the Regimental Drums of the Seaforth Highlanders which came proudly through the first World War; and the high walls bore the crests of many another Clan who had joined forces with MacKenzie and MacRae in some remembered cause.

Through dark stone passages and up shallow, winding stairs, I was then led to the upper floor, pausing to admire a beautifully carved oak door bearing the names of the successive Constables of Eilean Donan: MacRaes, Mathesons, Murchisons and Macaulays among others.

Each bedroom carries a name above its door—" Loch Long," " Eilean Donan," " Loch Duich " (the dark room which is lighted by only one tiny window at the head of stone stairs), and " Ballimore," from which one can enjoy a glorious view of the Black Cuillin. The walls of these bed-chambers are adorned by a variety of pictures—

water-colours of the Five Sisters, the burial-ground at Clachan Duich, the Castle before restoration. There are a few historical prints, among them one of the Battle of Glen Shiel, during the rising of 1719, when part of the Spanish forces fighting with the Highlanders had to retire to the top of Sgùrr Fhuaran, the highest of the Sisters, and remain there until their surrender next day. It was at this time, also, that the old Church of Kintail was destroyed, its minister being an ardent Jacobite.

I was also shown the old Castle gate, fished up in 1893 from the " Yellow Well " in the courtyard. This gate has since been copied, and its replica guards the entrance to the bridge.

Outside, on the ramparts, is the famous Murchison Stone, an immense boulder which was once lifted on to a wall in Glen Udalain by one man—John Murchison of Auchtertyre, one of the " Four Johns of Scotland," later killed at Sherriffmuir. This stone (the weight of which I could not begin to estimate), was afterwards conveyed to Ardelve by a certain Dugald Matheson, and thereafter removed, in 1932, to Eilean Donàn Castle at the instructions of Lt.-Col. MacRae-Gilstrap, the late Constable.

On the opposite side is the Clan MacRae War Memorial. Here, looking out from the grey rocks surrounding the Castle, haunted by the cries of sea-birds and the wailing of the wet wind blowing from the Isles, is a simple stone shrine bearing the names of MacRaes from all over the world who fell in the 1914-1918 War. Beneath the names is carved a quotation from the now-famous lines of Lt.-Col. John MacCrae:

> We are the dead. Short days ago,
> We lived, felt dawn, saw sunset glow,
> Loved and were loved. And now we lie
> In Flanders Fields . . .

The memorial is a replica of the stone seat erected to the poet's memory at Wimereux Cemetery, Flanders. And, somehow, one is made aware that though the dust of a thousand MacRaes might lie desolate in a foreign land, yet the spirit of every one of them would be here, among his own hills and the friends who have not forgotten . . .

I left Eilean Donan Castle reluctantly, with the feeling that I should return again to ramble through its gloomy passages and renew my acquaintance with its historic past. My mind was weighted down with its history and legend, and I came very near to envying Miss Macaulay her job!

As I crossed the bridge, the sun came out, filtering down through a broken sky. I stopped and looked back at the Castle. For a moment, it was washed over with pure gold.

Indeed, I thought, these old stones have taken on a new lease of life; and in their quiet, timeless way, are contributing much to a world so sorely in need of beauty.

CHAPTER IV

FINDING THE HILL-LOCHS

THE apple-blossoms were scattering on the grass. A few warm, heady days, and they had opened from waxen buds into a cloud of white wings, like a million rose-tipped butterflies settling on the gnarled twigs of the old black tree. Another day—and they were down in the dust, scattered and broken, their work accomplished, their supreme gesture to Beauty made—and ended.

They were blowing into the cottage; but, somehow, I had not the heart to sweep them up. By the morrow, they would be crinkled and withered on the polished floor. Until then, let them lie in their strange, forsaken loveliness, a memory of one enchanted hour. So sad —the days that are no more. So strange—the beautiful things of the world, that are always the shortest-lived. . .

The Spring was mellowing, and the long days of fine weather had returned. I had a wild desire to do something extra-ambitious— something no one in Kintail had thought of doing before. Getting out my map of Central Ross, I lay flat on the floor and brooded delightedly over the lines and contours—the green glens and thin blue streams; the brown mountains, each with its cap of white. At intervals in the high hills, tucked away in the dark curve of a corrie, a tiny blue pool marked a lochan. Some of these secret reservoirs were as high as three thousand feet, like shining jewels pinned against the breasts of the hills.

Suddenly, I had it! I would begin an article on " The Hill-Lochs of Kintail," visiting each of these little pools in turn, noting its height, surroundings, and the difficulty or otherwise of the ascent. Studying the map again, I realised that it would mean weeks of hard work, with even an occasional night on the hills, if I should miss my way or wander too far afield before dusk. Yet—it would be worth it! What opportunities would be mine of establishing contact with the real Kintail—the wild hill-country where only the shepherds and their collies ventured from one year's end to another! What breath-taking glimpses I would have of matchless mountain scenery, with the blue glens carving great chasms between range upon range of furrowed hills! What mad scrambles up heathery slopes and over treacherous scree to the forbidden fastnesses that hid the faery pools from my prying eyes! I started to count the number of exhausting tramps I should have to make before the article was finished—and gave it up. Most of them had names, which I read aloud to Jeannie, my tongue stumbling over the Gaelic, in which I am still far from proficient. I had the meanings, though—or most of them. Loch nan Ealachan—The Loch of the Swans. That would be a longish trip, though it would help if I cycled up to Glen Elchaig. I imagined the christening of this little lochan, the great white birds after which it was named swooping down out of a cloud-flecked sky, with the sunlight silvering their wings and the air vibrating with their strange, creaking flight. Loch a' Chléirich—the Loch of the Clerk (or Priest), an infinitesimal blue slit set high in the bosom of A' Ghlas-Bheinn, necessitating a steep climb up the course of a little burn. Loch an t-Sabhail—the Loch of the Barn—which I first carelessly translated as "The Loch of the Rescue," starting off an exciting train of thought—only to abandon it regretfully on a closer perusal of my dictionary. (I remembered how I had recently heard someone tell a story about a man who went fishing in one of the hill-lochs of the Highlands, and pulled out something so horrible that he dropped rod and line and took to his heels, and refused ever to say what he had caught! Could it be from some such monster as this that someone was once rescued up on the hill-lochs of Kintail?)

Thus enchanted, I passed an hour laying plans for my first trip. The next day, I arose early, packed up sandwiches, bade Jeannie a fond farewell, and set off on my cycle.

I pedalled through Dornie and over the brae towards Inverinate. On the edge of the village, I left my cycle by a grey stone bridge at the turn of the road, and started to follow An Leth Allt (The Half-Burn—probably at some time a boundary-line) up the deep gash of Coire Dhùinnid. The purling water fell in a series of small cascades, foaming into sunlit pools in which I could see small trout leaping as I passed. My goal was the aforementioned Loch an t-Sabhail and its next-door-neighbour, Loch nan Eun (The Loch of the Birds) on the plateau above Glen Elchaig. The day was ideal but with promise of great heat in the afternoon.

I meandered along the course of the stream, looking for the marked path. Several times I thought I had it—only to discover that I was on a sheep-track. (I found out later that it is much higher up, running along the side of the hill.) To my right, the vast bulk of Sgùrr an Airgid (the Hill of the Silver) shut out the hard blue sky, its rocks and streams shining in the sunlight, so that one could well understand how it got its name. On my left, green slopes patched with outcrops of rock ran up towards Boc Mór and Càrn Bad a' Chreamha.

After wandering for about three miles along the tree-clad pass, I found the path, a narrow, stony track that rose steadily into the hills. I passed a shepherd's hut and emerged into more open country—a large arena of heathery braes, loud with the bleating of sheep and the quavering echo of their new-born lambs. The hills became bleak and bare. I found the ruin of an old shieling, now a tumbled heap of grey stones, with only one wall standing. Under my feet, mica glinted among variegated pebbles. I noticed several odd varieties of moss, some pink and waxy, like coral, some resembling soft black velvet—and, of course, the water-logged sphagnum. Fantastic maps were drawn in blue, yellow, red and green lichen on the grey boulders by the wayside. The delicate sundew raised her red, sticky leaves out of black peat, and creeping azaleas peeped shyly above the rusty tufts of heather.

Climbing out of the maze of low hills at the end of the corrie, I had a fine view of the great ridge of Beinn Bhreac (Trout Hill), looking, indeed, very much like a fish, with sloping shelves of rock forming fins along his sides. Looking back, I could see Coire Dhùinnid, for the first time, to advantage—a deep cleft between the tumbled mass of Sgùrr an Airgid and the thrust-up snout of Boc Mór, the Big Roebuck.

I now lost the track among boulders and black, soggy peat-bog. I stumbled on, and emerged on to a wide plateau of brown and grey wasteland, bejewelled with many little black lochans, like sheets of polished ebony among the sombre moss and heather. I could see the crests of hills overlooking Glen Elchaig—Sgùman Cóinntich (not nearly so fierce from this angle), and the rounded top of Càrnan Cruineachd, on a level with my eyes.

I found Loch an t-Sabhail, desolate and dark with peat. There was not a sound, or a living creature in sight. The only sign that living things did, occasionally, come this way was some deer-tracks on the black fringes of the loch. It was sombre enough for me to start looking for monsters, so I mentally shook myself and hastened on to Loch nan Eun, whose name attracted me rather more. This loch is larger, and set in a welter of wild hill-tops, a dark mirror reflecting the grey, scorched rock of the Càrn behind. There are some little islands, as bleak and barren as their surroundings. I had hoped to swim out to the nearer, and largest, one—but one look at the water, oily black and full of bright, slimy weeds, made me change my mind. There was not a tree in sight, and I did not see one bird! Despite the brilliant sunlight, the landscape remained a sombre pattern of brown, black and grey, relieved only by the shining lochans and weirdly-tinted tufts of moss.

I turned back at last. It was tea-time, and I had had nothing to eat or drink since breakfast, acting on the principle that one should always get the climbing over first. I made my way down to the friendly rocks and trees of Coire Dhùinnid, and ate my "lunch" beside one of the many lovely linns. I filled my drinking-cup several times from the fast-flowing burn, and drank deeply of the clear golden water. Then, much refreshed, I resumed the homeward path.

The power had now gone out of the sun, and I enjoyed the tramp back to my cycle. In passing, I noticed that the bracken was beginning to uncurl on the slopes of the lower hills.

Loch nan Eun is quite an easy scramble, as a good path runs all but the last mile. Both it and Loch an t-Sabhail are set at roughly 1500 feet above sea-level. Despite its name, I have never visited a place more bleak and desolate, or more devoid of life. I can only conclude that the birds it was named after were buzzards!

A few days later, we looked at the map again and chose another fairly near one—the unnamed pool on the top of sprawling Beinn a' Mheadhoin (The Middle Hill), with its little sister hard by.

We were late starting, but had no particular need to hurry. This one was near enough for me to take Jeannie, and very happy she was at the prospect of chasing young rabbits on the hills.

We tramped along to Bundalloch and crossed the River Glennan by the stout wooden bridge. The sun blazed down on us out of a clear sky. Taking our time about it, we began working steadily up the spread-out, lumpy hill with its many hummocks and summits. While we were taking our first rest at the top of a rise, a cuckoo flew slowly past, quite close, giving its monotonous yet lovely cry. I watched its awkward, fluttering flight across the deep valley of the Glennan. Behind us, Loch Long was quiet and remote, unruffled by even a breath of moving air. Loch Alsh curved away to Beinn na Caillich, with a misty suggestion of the Cuillin beyond. There was a thick heat-haze over the high hills.

We climbed on, without haste. About half-way up the hill, we came on to a wide, grassy shelf, with another ridge of high cliffs behind. On this shelf we found the crumbling ruin of an old bothy!

I scanned the rock-face beyond, and once more consulted my map. Soon, we were climbing up a heathery chimney between two crags—a route I had planned from below.

Above this, we emerged on to the real plateau, the wild, uneven table-land which forms the top of the hill. Surrounded by humps and crags, we walked among the whitened bones of dead deer, scattered by the buzzards to the four winds. All around us, the tortured and riven face of the hill lay bared to the sky. This one hill is like a whole range of small mountains, and it occurred to me that it would be quite easy to get lost on the top should a mist descend.

As we tramped on over wet peat and springy heather, two grouse shot suddenly up from under our feet, shattering the silence with their harsh laughter. Though cock and hen, they cunningly flew off in opposite directions. An early dragonfly flashed past like a shooting star. Little pale brown moths flitted noiselessly over the darker brown of the heather.

We followed the long upward curve of the corrie, an easy walk, though somewhat wet underfoot. The cotton-wool heads of the canna trembled in the warm air, looking for all the world like snow-flakes balanced on thin black wires. The butterwort was in bloom, its deep mauve head demurely downcast on the top of a long green stem. It looked so innocent—until one peered closely at the sticky yellow leaves, where tiny flies struggled in the cruel embrace of the lovely sorceress who had enticed them to their doom.

Coming over the rise at the end of the corrie, I was brought to a sudden halt. The heather-slope ran steeply down into a hollow—and there was the loch, dark blue and as smooth as a sheet of Bristol glass. Behind it, serrated grey cliffs ran up into a maze of big hummocks, shining in the sunlight. Beyond these, the crest of Sgùman Còinntich towered up into the hazy sky. Away to the south were grotesque

Boc Mór, Càrn Bad a' Chreamha, and the hills I had seen previously from the summit of Coire Dhùinnid.

"As the crow flies," Loch Beinn a' Mheadhoin is about four miles to the north-west of Loch nan Eun. Though its name is less inspiring, it is infinitely more lovely. The bed of the loch is stony, and the water, instead of being black with peat, is quite clear and safe for a swim. I counted only four lonely little trees; but even these, in their bright green Spring dresses, added more than a hint of sylvan loveliness to the already lovely scene. The surrounding hills with their outcrops of shiny rock were so placed as to shelter the loch from sun and wind. The water was deep blue, shading to black where it reflected the majestic contours of the hills. Looking westward, I could see the pale mountains beyond Glen Udalain, their sunlit flanks glinting mysteriously through the blue haze.

Jeannie and I scrambled down the brae, and followed the loch round the curve at the far end. A few feet further, and we could see down to the far fringes of Killilan, the sweep of the River Elchaig, and the erratic course of the River Ling, zig-zagging away towards Meall Ruadh and the peak of Beinn Dronnaig, accompanied by the white ribbon of the road.

We returned to the loch, found a smooth, warm rock, and ate our lunch at the edge of the sparkling water. Trout began to jump like flashes of silver fire in the sunlight. Jeannie threw herself flat in the heather and closed her eyes. Only the occasional twitching of a paw or ear betrayed the fact that she was alive.

Little puffs of cloud drifted across a powder-blue sky. The sun fell warmly on my face and shoulders. I scanned the landscape. Not a soul in sight. I was alone in the youth of the world. Just so, I thought, must the young gods have felt, before Pandora opened the box of troubles. Fragments of poetry drifted through my mind. The Chorus from *Atalanta in Calydon*—snatches of Keats, and songs of Greece, whose authorship I had forgotten. Time slipped back and back to the days of the chariot and the laurel-wreath—the flash of sandalled feet and lissome limbs—the echo of golden laughter in the woods of Arcady. O vanished age of beauty, whose culture is but a breath of perfume from the past! And did the same white clouds float over Ithaca—the same soft and scented breezes touch Olympus, moving the high gods to tears . . . ?

The laughter died; the shadows fled. Time tripped back into far, misty realms of space. Now there was no knowledge or culture—just the green of primeval forests, and the striving of life after light. Once more, I was alone, a pagan in a pagan world, wherein only a dream of beauty moved forward to its preconceived end. . .

I undressed, and lay flat on the warm rock, giving myself up to the caresses of Apollo. Small insects sailed over me on lazy, transparent wings. Only the fret of a silver fin in the water, the intermittent croaking of a frog, broke a silence heavier than the weight of the years.

And then, a tiny sound stirred across my consciousness—a soft, regular throbbing, calling me back from the far fringes of time. Like a little heart beating, the rhythmic tick of my wrist-watch shattered the spell, reminding me that I was not, and never could be, alone . . . Instinctively, I reached for my clothes.

A huge, pale-coloured bird flapped slowly across the sky. With the aid of the binoculars, I saw that it was a creamish-white, with brown flecks. From its size, it must have been one of the larger birds of prey, but I could not identify it at that distance. Slowly, like a vanishing dream, it sailed away into the blue haze—and it was somehow symbolic of an age of beauty glimpsed for a moment and then lost forever.

I sat up and drew my bare toes out of the water. Even in that short time, my shoulders had caught the sun, and I could hardly bear the touch of my jacket.

Calling to the reluctant Jeannie, who awakened slowly from some deep dream of her own, I set off over the heather, having decided to find the second loch marked—but still unnamed—on my map.

It was much nearer than I had imagined. So near, in fact, that at first I missed the route, and came out over the dizzy cliffs above the valley of the Glennan. Looking down at the river was like peering over the edge of the world. Across the deep blue gash, the hills opposite were a wonderful panorama of grey precipices and heathery slopes, broken by the courses of dried-up streams. The steepness of those cliffs turned my knees to water.

I drew back somewhat abruptly, and trudged on over whispering canna, bearing now to my right. Presently, I found the loch, which is small and desolate and not nearly so inspiring as its neighbour. I did not even see a fish jump—though doubtless there were many in the depths of the still, dark water. The one redeeming feature of the landscape here was a splendid view of Sgùman Cóinntich peeping over a decline between the hills.

There is an interesting story about this loch, though, which was told to me by Mr. Donald MacRae of Bundalloch. During the days of the "whisky smuggling" (as illegal distilling was called in the Highlands), the old crumbling bothy half-way up Beinn a' Mheadhoin was a favourite haunt of the smugglers. Donald MacRae's grandmother, whose house stood on the same site as his own, was one day looking out of her door while the men were away "on the hill." Suddenly she saw a party of gaugers coming along the road in the distance. Swiftly, she ran up the steep hillside to the old bothy, where two men and a woman were busily engaged in an occupation common at that time among the Highlanders. Quickly, the warning was passed on, and the still and equipment carried up the hill and hidden in the little loch. The keg of newly-distilled spirit was pushed under an overlapping ridge of heather just beside the bothy (there wasn't time to do more), and the two women then sat on it, covering it with their skirts. When the inspectors arrived, they drew a complete blank!

Beinn a' Mheadhoin is a hill of infinite variety. The ascent to the lochs took me just over an hour, going easily and enjoying every moment of the way. If one avoids the rocky patches, it is an easy scramble, and the scenery well repays the visitor for his exertions.

My third choice was a tramp in search of the hill-lochs around Boc Mór, still quite near at hand and easy of access. This, I felt, would complete a cycle, for I should have then " covered " all the hill-lochs on the range immediately above Loch Duich and Loch Long.

After waiting until one-thirty for the weather to decide what it was going to do, I took a chance, packed up some tea, and got out my long-suffering cycle.

I rode quickly down to Dornie, and left my cycle in a ruined bothy at Carndu. Wasting as little time as possible, I started off up the hillside.

Behind me, Loch Long fell away into a blue hollow. Soon, I could enjoy a lovely view of the Cuillin, spread out like a relief-map on the western horizon. From this angle, I could get a much better idea of the distance between the peaks. One or two of them were streaked with new snow as a result of several days of low temperature and biting wind. Over the whole range, heavy cloud was clustered in soft waves of grey and white, spilling down here and there into the corries and clefts between. It was a day of fitful sunshine and a sharp, cold breeze blowing off the sea. Thin blue veils of rain—or sleet—were drifting over the northern hills.

At about 1500 feet, I attained a stretch of flat peat-bog from which, in every direction, I could see the hills rolling away into the clouds, splashed with great patches of golden light. There was new snow on the crests of the Five Sisters and the high hills overlooking Glen Shiel. Away to the west, the sky was a soft, watery blue, with great bands of cumulus cloud hanging like cotton-wool over the Cuillin and the white-flecked sea. Loch Duich, far below, was in deep shadow;

LOCH ALSH, SKYE HILLS ON THE HORIZON, FROM KYLE OF LOCHALSH

but over and beyond Glen Udalain the landscape was washed over with a faint greenish-gold.

The wind whipped me, and I could not stay still for long. I tramped on over newly-burnt heather, looking for some of the many small lochans marked on my map.

Presently, I surmounted the corrie behind Creag Réidh Raineach (The Smooth Crag of the Bracken—though nary a bit did I see!) From here, I could see as far north as the hills beyond Glen Carron— a wonderful tapestry of grey and gold, splashed with waves of dark blue where the cloud-shadows moved softly over ben and corrie.

I was now entering a wilderness of desolate grey crags and precipices, to which not even the sunlight could give life or colour. On the fringe of this upheaved and tortured land, I found Loch Gorm, the Blue Loch, the first of a chain of three small lochans. It was, indeed, of a bluish colour, but very desolate in its stark and savage surroundings, two infinitesimal islands being its only concession to the picturesque.

The second loch in the chain boasted a fringe of pale green grasses, looking at their reflections in the cold waters. The third, over a slight rise, was an irregular pool backed by heathery crags, with a fine view of the Glen Shiel hills beyond.

I climbed another rise, to the east this time. Suddenly, I came upon a small herd of deer, quite close by. I stopped dead, and we stared at each other. Obviously, they did not know what to make of me. My note-book flickered, and they moved off. I moved away from them—and they came back again, wide-eyed with curiosity! For a moment, I had them silhouetted on a high ridge, black against the skyline—lovely, delicate creatures of unbelievable grace. Then they disappeared without haste over the brow of the hill.

I went on, and found Loch Dubh (the Black Loch) and its little satellite lochan, set amid a tumble of grey crags, dark with the reflections of barren cliffs in their waters.

"And now," I thought, " for Loch Bhuic Mhóir,"—which was the one I had come particularly to see.

Before me, the bulk of the Big Roebuck rose like a huge clenched fist against the sky. I decided to get an unusual slant on its loch, so I climbed up its round, ugly face to the tiny pimple of the cairn. I was now 2064 feet up, the highest I had been so far in my search for the hill-lochs of Kintail. Below me, on the far side of the hill, Loch Bhuic Mhóir, completely devoid of islands or trees, lay dark and still in a dull brown hollow. It is a larger loch than any in the two " chains," but has absolutely no distinguishing features.

But I could not regret climbing Boc Mór! There, around me, in every direction, was a view of hills and hill-lochs which stole my breath away. This hill, standing alone and towering above a maze of lower eminences, is a splendid vantage-point from which to survey the whole of the range. I could see the two lochs on the top of Beinn a' Mheadhoin, and the chain of silver pools I had lately left. Gleaming among the nearer western hills were the lochs above Sallachy and Conchra—Loch Anna, Loch Ainn na Gaibhre and an unnamed pool sheltering darkly among great, sheer cliffs in a hollow devoid of light.

I walked round the summit of the Big Roebuck, revelling in the view. Now I could pick out some of the hill-lochs on the other side of Loch Duich, above Letterfearn—and many another shiny lochan nestling among the hill-tops, unnamed and unmarked on my map.

I cannot leave this scene without some especial mention of the hills themselves. I looked out across high peaks capped with untrodden snow; and all about me, crag upon grey crag, fold upon brown fold, the heaped-up mountains of Kintail lay bared to a cloud-strewn sky.

And then—the islands! Loch Alsh, running out towards the dying sun. Eilean Bàn, with its white lighthouse, at the gateway to the Sound. Pabay, Scalpay, little Longay, the Crowlin Islands, the long line of Raasay, all clinging round the skirts of Skye. I could see

Broadford Bay—and there, between Scalpay and Raasay, the beginnings of Loch Sligachan curving away into the high hills of Eilean a' Cheò.

I had my tea in the shelter of the summit-cairn. I felt I could have stayed for ever, looking down on to this wonderland spread out like a faery map at my feet.

The light was going out of the landscape, though, and the biting wind had begun to draw little wrinkles across the grey face of the distant waters.

Regretfully, I shouldered my pack and began the long descent, trudging steadily down through gathering shadows towards the gleam of white houses below.

CHAPTER V

THE LOVELIEST GLEN IN THE WEST HIGHLANDS ?

STRICTLY speaking, Glen Shiel is no longer part of Kintail. In fact, the two parishes were separated as far back as 1726. No book on the district would be complete, however, without a mention of this wild and lovely glen running away through great, dark pinnacles to Loch Cluanie and far Glen Moriston. Indeed, from every aspect except the parochial one, Glen Shiel and Kintail are bound together by indissoluble bonds. Their history, tradition and folklore are so closely-linked as to be intermingled—and as for their geography— well, it would be impossible to imagine Kintail without her Five Sisters, which are, oddly enough, in the parish of Glen Shiel!

So I am including this historic glen in my Kintail Scrapbook without so much as an apology—and I will even go so far as to say that anyone who visits Kintail and omits to wander at least half-way along Glen Shiel has missed one of the finest attractions the district has to offer.

In old documents, the three main glens of Kintail are given as Glen Elchaig, Glen Shiel and Glen Lichd, and it is noted that at one time the " steep and lofty mountains " surrounding these three glens were frequently covered with green pasture from the base almost to the summit. So fine, indeed, were these grazing-grounds that Kintail was known of old as Cintaille nam Bó, or Kintail of the cows. After the '45, when cattle-reiving and clan feuds came to an end, this whole district enjoyed a period of great prosperity (as distinct from other parts of the Highlands, where conditions worsened steadily until the famine of 1782).

In Kintail and Glen Shiel, this period and the remainder of the century saw the heyday of the " Shieling," when lads and lasses would spend whole summers up in the hills with the cattle, erecting huts for sleeping accommodation and leading, generally, a merry and carefree life to the accompaniment of song, laughter and love-making. Later, the lands were sold, the young men emigrated, extensive sheep-farming took the place of the Highland cattle, and the old days of prosperity were at an end. From that time, the population steadily decreased, chiefly due to the emigration of people who could not adjust themselves to the new ideas, or whose holdings had been assimilated into the large-scale farms.

With regard to the rich pasture-lands it is still possible to visualise these on the hills of Glen Elchaig and Glen Lichd; but Glen Shiel is another matter. A great deal of the surface of the peaks on either side is scree and boulders, and one can only conclude here that the cattle would have been better advised to stay in the green and fertile valley.

My first long cycle-ride into the heart of this deep, dark glen was made on a day of sun, cloud and a high wind—as usual, dead against me! Having fought my way along the side of Loch Duich, I found temporary shelter under the hills at Morvich, where I was able to stop and regain a little of my breath. At this point, some fellow-cyclists passed me, two young men and a girl, puffing and sweating up the hill while I stood still and surveyed the landscape. One of the young men, naked to the waist, was a rich golden colour, including his hair, as if he just stepped out of the cast of *Ben Hur*. They looked at me rather enviously as I stood taking what I considered to be a hard-earned rest, but did not emulate my example.

From where I stood, I had an excellent view, across the head of Loch Duich, of the Dùnan Diarmaid, that great mound just beyond the ruined burial-ground of Clachan Duich, where it is said that " Diarmid the Beautiful " was buried, together with his galley and personal possessions, after his ill-fated encounter with the wild boar in Kintail forest. Diarmid, according to the legend, was the lover of Fingal's wife, Grainne—though not necessarily of his own choice. It was the custom in those days for a lady, if she so wished, to put " geasan " (or an obligation) on a man to fulfil her dearest desire. It was a point of honour that the man should not refuse. Grainne, attracted by Diarmid's comeliness, put " geasan " on him to carry her off on the day of her marriage to Fingal, after the wedding-feast—which act the hero performed successfully, to his own undoing. Fingal accomplished his revenge in a deadly and cunning manner. Pretending friendship towards Diarmid, he organised a hunt into Kintail forest to slay a savage wild boar which had long devastated the district. This boar had a poisonous bristle in its hide, and Fingal was hoping that the encounter would prove to be a fatal one for Diarmid, but the opposite proved to be the case. Diarmid returned safe and sound, having accomplished the task without injury to himself. Fingal then made a wager with him about the length of the boar, and asked him to go back and measure it from head to tail. This, also, Diarmid did —but Fingal professed himself dissatisfied, and requested Diarmid to measure it again, from tail to snout. It was while doing this that Diarmid pricked his heel on the poisonous bristle. As he lay dying, he begged Fingal to go and get him a drink from a nearby well. Fingal, however, tarried until it was too late. When at last he went to the well, Diarmid was past his help. The well, a little above Dorusduain, is called Tobar an Tuirc, the Well of the Boar. It is said that Fingal, greatly repented of his act after the hero's death, and Diarmid was buried with all honour.

Another version of this old tale was recounted to me by Dr. Farquhar MacRae of Ratagan, a tall, stately gentleman of ninety-two, with a hand-grip of iron and a ready smile for the stranger. Grainne, he explained, was the daughter of the King of the Cuillins, and Fingal's second wife. She fell in love with Diarmid because of certain beauty-spots on his face which made him irresistible to women. At first, he struggled against his fate, declaring that he would not have her either indoors or outdoors—whereupon she placed herself on the threshold, neither in nor out, and so cunningly overcame his objection! When Fingal decreed the hunt, the Fingalians gathered behind Inverinate, and the boar ran into Glen Lichd, closely pursued by Diarmid and one other. In lungeing at the boar, Diarmid split an immense boulder with his spear—and at once water gushed out, forming the well which is still in existence to-day. After he had slain the boar, the length of it was found to be sixteen feet. As the hero lay dying, he asked for a drink from the "shell of virtue," which was reputed to cure all ills. This, however, Fingal refused him. Diarmid then died—and, a little later, the heartbroken Grainne died too, followed by her two beautiful hounds. In great remorse, Fingal buried them all in the same grave, and afterwards expressed his regret at killing his sister's only son for a woman who no longer loved him.

The grave was marked with a mound and a double row of stones. Dr. Farquhar MacRae told me how it was once opened—but nothing was found except one clay pot. It was later thought that the excavations were not deep enough.

The tragic story of Diarmid and Grainne is told briefly and eloquently in Dr. MacRae's original poem, *Kintail*, the whole of which I am here quoting, with his permission:

Now here's to my bonnie Kintail—
    Its corries, its clachans, its cairns;
And here's to its rivers, all teeming forever
    With salmon that flash on the wave!

And here's to the Sisters who reign
    O'er moorland and mountain and main,
And lavish their bounty on field and on fountain
    And give to our county its fame!

And here's to Loch Duich, I hold
    Most peerless of lochs to behold;

At evening when placid it mirrors Beinn Fhada
And Sisters all mantled in gold!

And here's to brave Diarmid o' Doone,
    Who sleeps with Finn's queen in yon tomb,
And her beautiful pets, that died of regrets,
    Keeping watch at their feet until doom.

Many localities, of course, claim the story of the Fingalian boar-hunt as their own—which only proves the extent to which these old legends once captured and held the imagination of the Highlander.

Glenelg, which contains three Pictish brochs, is said to be the burial-place of many of Fingal's warriors, and stories are told of enormous bones being ploughed up in the fields, and great tempests arising when the graves of the giants were inadvertently disturbed.

The country around Glenelg was also celebrated for cattle-reiving, and Dr. Farquhar MacRae told me the story of a great hero of Kintail, Eonachan Dubh, or Little Black John, who once outwitted the Lochaber raiders and recovered a valuable herd of cattle single-handed. The story goes that Eonachan Dubh came upon the reivers at night, and found them all in a hut with the stolen cattle grazing outside. He went in and made friends with them—then presently went out again and shouted that the cattle had all disappeared. When one of the Lochaber men came out to see for himself, Little Black John, under cover of the dark, overpowered him—and two more were served likewise. He then called on the remaining two men to surrender, and sent them all, gagged and bound, with his compliments, back to Lochiel, while he himself collected the scattered cattle and drove them back to pasture.

It was this same hero who, being friendly with Seaforth, and a frequent visitor to Brahan Castle, took it upon himself to reprove the Countess for her extravagance in insisting upon cinnamon fires and a fresh ox-tongue every day of the year.

THE LOVELIEST GLEN IN THE WEST HIGHLANDS?

I cannot leave Dr. Farquhar MacRae without recounting a delightful story concerning one of his ancestors, an old woman who lived near Lienassie. When Cromwell's men were in Kintail, one of them broke into this old lady's house and, finding her alone by the fire, attempted to snatch a large silver brooch from her neck. She, however, promptly grabbed his outstretched hand in a grip so fierce that she dislocated his thumb! He then tried to kick her—but the intrepid lady seized his foot and threw him backwards into the ashes! When he protested to his captain, this officer simply shrugged and said: " Serve you right! You had no business with the old woman and her brooch! "

Later, the old lady's son had a drinking-cup made from the brooch, and it has been a treasured family heirloom ever since. The son was Dr. MacRae's great-great-grandfather, and the cup (as I was able to see for myself) is now in the doctor's possession.

But I must on to Glen Shiel, and my adventures on the windy afternoon when I resolved to pry into its dark secrets.

The road ran on between the high peaks of the Five Sisters on the east, and the sharp, jagged, nearly-black ridge of the Saddle opposite.

Still fighting against the wind, and climbing steadily now all the time, I passed some Highland cattle and cream-coloured ponies, one with a tiny pale foal. Presently, I crossed a stone bridge and reached a point from whence I could look up into green Coire Mhalagain, zig-zagging up to the double point of Sgùrr na Sgìne, the Hill of the Sgian, or Dirk. It was at Achnasheal, near Malagan, that Dr. Johnson and the faithful Boswell were entertained to milk by the inhabitants of the glen. Here is Boswell's account of their ride through Glen Shiel:

We passed through Glensheal, with prodigious mountains on each side. We saw where the battle was fought in the year 1719. Dr. Johnson owned he was now in a scene of as wild nature as he could see . . .

KINTAIL PEAKS AND LOCH DUICH FROM INVERINATE

The good Doctor, however (with characteristic perversity) was not prepared to be carried away by the scenery to the extent of losing his critical faculties, for (says Boswell):

He corrected me sometimes in my inaccurate observations. "There," said I, " is a mountain like a cone."

Johnson. "No, sir. It would be called so in a book, but when a man comes to look at it he sees it is not so. It is indeed pointed at the top, but one side of it is larger than the other."

Another mountain I called immense.

Johnson. "No; it is no more than a considerable protruberance."

And then, continues Boswell:

We came to a rich green valley, comparatively speaking, and stopped a while to let our horses rest and eat grass. . .

Even Dr. Johnson seems to have been carried away by the scene at this point; for, in his *Journey to the Western Islands of Scotland* he describes it thus :

I sat down on a bank, such as a writer of romance might have delighted to feign. I had, indeed, no trees to whisper over my head; but a clear rivulet streamed at my feet. The day was calm, the air soft, and all was rudeness, silence, and solitude. Before me, and on either side, were high hills, which, by hindering the eye from ranging, forced the mind to find entertainment for itself. Whether I spent the hour well, I know not; for here I first conceived the thought of this narration.

After a rest in this quiet and lovely spot, the two travellers continued their ride to Achnasheal:

A kind of rural village. . . a number of cottages being built together, as we saw all along in the Highlands . . . At Auchnasheal, we sat down on a green turf seat at the end of a house; they brought us out two wooden dishes of milk, which we tasted. One of them was frothed like a syllabub. I saw a woman preparing it with such a stick as is used for chocolate, and in the same manner. We had a considerable circle about us, all Macraes, Lord Seaforth's people. Not one of them could speak English. I observed to Dr. Johnson it was much the same as being with a tribe of Indians. "Yes, sir; but not so terrifying." I gave all who chose it snuff and tobacco. Governor Trapaud had made us buy a quantity at Fort Augustus, and put them up in small parcels. I also gave each person a bit of wheat bread, which they had never tasted before. I then gave a penny a-piece to each child. I told Dr. Johnson of this; upon which he called to Joseph and our guides for change for a shilling, and declared that he would distribute among the children. Upon this being announced in Erse there was a great stir; not only did some children come running down from neighbouring huts, but I observed one black-haired man, who had been with us all along, had gone off, and returned, bringing a very young child. My fellow-traveller then ordered the children to be drawn up in a row; and he dealt about his copper, and made them and their parents all happy. The poor Macraes, whatever may be their present state, were of considerable estimation in the year 1715 . . .

There is a footnote here, added by Boswell at a later date, touching the celebrated "Affair of the MacRaes" in 1778, when a company of Seaforth's men, due to embark for Jersey and the East Indies mutinied and encamped for three days and nights on Arthur's Seat, above Edinburgh, refusing to come down until their commanders had explained matters to their satisfaction.

Boswell cites this episode as an instance of the " spirited exertions " of which the men of Kintail were, on occasion, capable.

His description of the inhabitants of Glen Shiel, and their manners, follows in these words:

There was great diversity in the faces of the circle around us: some were as black and wild in their appearance as any American savages whatever. One woman was as comely almost as the figure of Sappho, as we see it painted. We asked the old woman, the mistress of the house where we had the milk (which, by the bye, Dr. Johnson told me, for I did not observe it myself, was built not of turf but of stone), what we should pay. She said, " what we pleased." One of our guides asked her in Erse if a shilling was enough. She said " Yes "; but some of the men bade her ask more. This vexed me, because it showed a desire to impose upon strangers, as they knew that even a shilling was high payment. The woman, however, honestly persisted in her first price, so I gave her half-a-crown; thus we had one good scene of life uncommon to us. The people were very much pleased, gave us many blessings and said, " they had not had such a day since the old Laird of Macleod's time."

Johnson's own account of the journey through Glen Moriston and Glen Shiel provides an interesting contrast in style—and, incidentally, reveals the fundamental differences in character and outlook between the two travellers—the shallow, chatty, humorous Boswell;

and the staid, philosophic doctor with his innate dread of over-statement. Approaching Loch Cluanie, he writes:

Of the hills, which our journey offered to the view on either side, we did not take the height, nor did we see any that astonished us with their loftiness. Towards the summit of one there was a white spot, which I should have called a naked rock, but the guides, who had better eyes, and were acquainted with the phenomena of the country, declared it to be snow. It had already lasted to the end of August, and was likely to maintain its contest with the sun till it should be reinforced by winter. . .

Of the hills many may be called, with Homer's *Ida*, " abundant in springs," but few can deserve the epithet which he bestows upon Pelion by " waving their leaves." They exhibit very little variety; being almost wholly covered with dark heath, and even that seems to be checked in its growth. What is not heath is nakedness, a little diversified by now and then a stream rushing down the steep. An eye accustomed to flowery pastures and waving harvests is astonished and repelled by this wide extent of hopeless sterility. . .

We were in this place at ease and by choice, and had no evils to suffer or to fear; yet the imaginations excited by the view of an unknown and untravelled wilderness are not such as arise in the artificial solitude of parks and gardens, a flattering notion of self-sufficiency, a placid indulgence of voluntary delusions, a secure expansion of the fancy, or a cool concentration of the mental powers. The phantoms which haunt a desert are want and misery and danger; the evils of dereliction rush upon the thoughts; man is made unwillingly acquainted with his own weakness, and meditation shows him only how little he can sustain, and how little he can perform. There were no traces of inhabitants, except perhaps a rude pile of clods called a summer hut, in which a herdsmen had rested in the favourable seasons. Whoever had been in the place where I then sat, unprovided with provisions and ignorant of the country, might, at least before the roads were made, have wandered among the rocks, till he had perished with hardship, before he could have found either food or shelter. Yet what are these hillocks to the ridges of Taurus, or these spots of wildness to the deserts of America?

After passing Loch Cluanie (" kept full by many streams ") the good doctor describes his meeting with the Macraes in Glen Shiel.

The loch at last ended in a river broad and shallow like the rest, but that it may be passed when it is deeper there is a bridge over it. Beyond it is a valley called Glenshiel, inhabited by the clan Macrae. Here we found a village called Auchnashiels, consisting of many huts, perhaps twenty, built all of dry stones, that is, stones piled up without mortar. . . The people of this valley did not appear to know any English, and our guides now became doubly necessary as interpreters. A woman, whose hut was distinguished by greater spaciousness and better architecture, brought out some pails of milk. The villagers gathered about us in considerable numbers, I believe without any evil intention, but with a very savage wildness of aspect and manner. . . Mr. Boswell sliced the bread, and divided it amongst them, as he supposed them never to have tasted a wheaten loaf before. . .

But I shall be in trouble among my Highland friends if I give so much space to Johnson and Boswell and forbear to mention another, and more illustrious, visitor to Glen Shiel! Prince Charles Edward, following the ancient road over the Bealach Dubh Leac on his way from Loch Hourn to Strathglass, spent the night of July 27th, 1746, with five followers, in a cave above Malagan when a party of soldiers passed down the glen. This cave is still pointed out, as is also a large boulder known as " The Prince's Stone."

The men of Kintail and Glen Shiel were, for the most part, Jacobites; though it is on record that the Earl of Seaforth supported the House of Hanover. Many of the young men ran away to join the army of the Prince—and tradition has it that none of them ever returned. There is a popular story about one Farquhar MacRae who resembled the Prince so strongly that he contrived to get himself mistaken for Charles about two days after the Prince had been reported to be hiding in Kintail. He was arrested by the King's soldiers and taken to Fort William, whence his mother finally came to identify him, and so secured his release. Whether his arrest was accomplished by design, to draw off the pursuit from its real objective, or whether it was accidental, remains a mystery—though the young man in question was known to be a staunch Jacobite.

Glen Shiel has connections with the Stuart cause which date from the time of Charles I. Seaforth, it is true, fought against Montrose at Auldearn in 1645—but it was said that he deliberately allowed Montrose an easy victory. Shortly afterwards, he publicly declared himself a supporter of the King, and from then onwards the people of Kintail and Glen Shiel stood almost unanimously for the ill-starred Stuarts until

after Culloden. During the rising of 1715, they suffered heavy losses
at Sherriffmuir, as has previously been recounted in the chapter on the
Castle of Eilean Donan. At the time of the Castle's destruction, in
1719, a fierce battle was fought in Glen Shiel, at a place thereafter called
Eas-nan-arm, or the Waterfall of the Arms. At first, the Highlanders
stood firm, reinforced by Spanish troops sent by Cardinal Alberoni.
Then the heather caught fire, and Seaforth was wounded. The Highlanders fell into confusion and retreated to the mountains. The
Spaniards, not knowing the country, ended up on the fierce pinnacles
of the Five Sisters—according to some accounts on Sgùrr Fhuaran,
and to others on Sgùrr nan Spainteach. The site of the battle is still
easily located. Trenches are visible on both sides of the ravine at the
narrowest part of the valley. Above the higher fall, a ghost is seen
at this spot—the image of a Dutch colonel killed in the battle by a
rifleman with a sixpence—a deadly missile to those with charmed lives.
Rob Roy was rumoured to be a spectator of the battle, and so were
the Chisholms, who viewed the action from Bealach a' Laphain (the
Fainting Pass) up in the hills. I was told by a local inhabitant that
Eas-nan-Arm was said to be the place where the Highlanders buried
their arms rather than let them fall into the hands of their foes.

Touching the matter of the " ghost," I certainly felt an eeriness,
a sense of something outside time, about this part of the glen. All
around me, the great, dark hills blocked out the sky, as if reluctant to
allow me to emerge from the gloom of their wild and lovely demesne.
Beyond the Bridge of Shiel, water was cascading down the braes over
grey aprons of stone, on its way to join the main stream. Looking
back, I gazed into a deep cleft flanked by black peaks rising in sombre
beauty against a stormy sky. I should not have been surprised to
hear the wild skirl of pipes, and meet a company of tattered Highlanders
coming along the road!

Much of the battle-site is now overgrown with young plantations
of larch and pine. I passed wave upon wave of infant trees, all clothed

in vivid green. The broom was tossing its yellow butterfly-blossoms in the wind. I found one or two ruined crofts, and faint traces of General Wade's old road running along at the feet of the hills. Under a greystone bridge, sea-pinks were in flower among wet slabs of rock.

I struggled on to the water-shed where Glen Shiel meets Glen Cluanie, and the two rivers run side by side down the green hills opposite, wending through steep corries softened by silver birches, then swinging apart in the glen and going their separate ways. Though still in the " parish," I had now, properly speaking, reached the head of Glen Shiel, so I allowed the wind to have its way at last, and turned back. Another day, I would follow the road through Glen Cluanie to the loch—and maybe on to Glen Moriston, God willing.

The return journey was a refreshing change—down-hill practically all the way, with the gale pushing me so hard that I had both hands on the brakes. I was able—nay, compelled—to jolt along at a colossal speed all the way to the little loch at the mouth of Glen Shiel, with no incident but a threatened collision with a long-horned black-faced ram who stood in the road like the Rock of Gibraltar and waited to see which of us would come off worse!

I stopped at the loch, and sat on a low grey wall to have my tea. Quite fearlessly, three heron emerged from the reeds and began dipping their orange bills among the pale strands of weed, their graceful lines reflected in the clear water. A pair of oyster-catchers flew off, laughing shrilly across the silence; and a mallard alighted with a soft splash and skimmed along like a sea-plane, shattering the surface of the loch into a million ripples and particles of flying foam. Right out into the deeper water, fringe upon fringe of blue-green grasses bent and bowed to the song of the wind, quieter here because of the close-sheltering hills.

Meandering out of this deep, lovely glen, I fought the wind again through Invershiel and Morvich, until it was once more behind me as I sped along the far shore of Loch Duich towards Inverinate. Here,

I kept a sharp look-out for the slow-worms which are often basking on this road on sultry evenings. Though I am not prepossessed with the appearance of this particular reptile (it being altogether too much like a snake for my liking), I would rather pick one up with my bare hands than run over it.

It was late when I reached Dornie—later still when I arrived at the cottage. I was tired and battered from fighting against the wind—but the sombre glory of Glen Shiel had put its spell upon me, and I knew that I should soon return.

Here, to digress for a moment from the main subject of this chapter. I *did* return, not many days later—and this time I got a lift in a car and went right through Glen Cluanie and Glen Moriston, a distance of some forty miles. During the whole journey, rain fell in sheets from the grey sky and rose in sheets from under the speeding wheels. The hills were a misty pattern of blues and greys, the higher peaks hidden behind curtains of drifting cloud. I had planned to climb up to some hill-lochs above Loch Cluanie (still in the parish of Glen Shiel), but changed my mind as the weather showed no least sign of improving.

Beyond the water-shed, the hills became rocky and barren—a no-man's land of desolate, dark hummocks, the monotonous brown and grey of heather and rock broken only by the gleam of yellow, swollen waters surging over great slabs of stone set in the flanks of the hills. Soon, the Tomdoun road swung away to the right.

We passed Loch Beag and two half-drowned hikers. A short distance along the shore of Loch Cluanie, the car broke down with water in the engine! No sooner was this fixed than it broke down again with a flat tyre at the back! It was definitely "one of those days."

My companions changed the wheel with amazing cheerfulness.

STORM CLOUDS ABOVE GLEN SHIEL FROM INVERINATE

Meantime, I occupied myself looking out of the streaming windows at Loch Cluanie, a long, spread-out strip of dull grey water set among sparsely-forested hills. Maybe it was the day, but what I saw failed to impress me.

When we reached the River Moriston, however, the scene changed. For those who prefer the sylvan to the stark type of scenery, this glen is even lovelier than Glen Shiel. Certainly, it is more friendly. Even in teeming rain, the beauty of it is enough to make you catch your breath. On this particular day, the turbulent river, swollen by heavy cloudbursts, foamed and frothed along a grey gorge, between dark islands set with young vegetation. Here and there, a black pool swirled slowly round and round in some secret bay or cove, with the yellow foam piling high as it drifted in from the main current. And all around were trees, trees—bright feathery folds of shining green— oak and gold-tasselled rowan; silver birch and twinkling poplar—larch, firs, and massive, tufted pines—clothing all the lovely, rock-strewn land in green robes of enchantment. Under the dripping foliage, small, star-like flowers shone white among green moss, and last year's leaves, brown and withered, traced many a random track into the heart of the forest, as if inviting the wanderer's feet.

It was at Anoch, in Glen Moriston—the inn run by a Highlander called Macqueen—that Johnson and Boswell obtained their first real insight into Highland life. The inn was later made into a farm, but at the time of their visit it was a well-known resting-place for the drovers of cattle going south from Skye. The landlord was of the old type of Highland gentleman—hospitable and well-educated in the Classics. He made the two travellers welcome, and, after dinner, told them of his life and circumstances. Boswell remarks on the wainscoted walls of the room, made " with wicker, very neatly plaited," done entirely with his own hands. The inn itself was " built of thick turfs and thatched with thinner turfs and heath; it had three rooms in length, and a little room which projected."

Boswell goes on to describe, in his inimitable way, how, after tea, Dr. Johnson had presented the inn-keeper's daughter, "a modest, civil girl, very neatly dressed," with a book he had bought in Inverness. This book, it appears, gave rise to no little discussion throughout the Highlands:

Several ladies, wishing to learn the kind of reading which the great and good Dr. Johnson esteemed most fit for young women, desired to know what book he had selected for this Highland nymph. "They never adverted," said he, "that I had no *choice* in the matter. I have said that I presented her with a book which I *happened* to have about me." And what was this book? My readers, prepare your features for merriment. It was *Cocker's Arithmetic*.

One day, Boswell ventured to ask Dr. Johnson why he had bought such a book at Inverness. He replied: "Why, sir, if you are to have but one book with you upon a journey, let it be a book of science. When you have read through a book of entertainment, you know it, and it can do no more for you; but a book of science is inexhaustible."

(How one regrets not seeing the face of the girl at the inn when the book was presented!)

We had tea at the Invermoriston Hotel, and I then said goodbye to my companions and set out on the long tramp back to Dornie. It was all of forty miles, and, as it was already four-thirty in the afternoon, I hardly dared to contemplate my plight should I fail to obtain a lift— especially as the Cluanie Bridge Inn was not at this time taking in visitors, having closed down in 1942, until further notice.

The rain had stopped, and I walked about eight miles through the sunlit woods, with Jeannie trotting at my heels. Then, just as the sky began to cloud over again, I had the good fortune to be picked up by a furniture-van. In the course of conversation with the driver, I regretted having omitted to see the "Footprints of Glen Moriston," which, I assumed, we had passed by that time. As it happened, we had not. The driver obligingly stopped the van at the appropriate place, and guided me along the path to the memorial cairn erected over this sacred spot. There, beside the rotting stump of an old tree, we stood looking down at the footprints, cut deep into smooth grass, plain as the day they were made. I knelt down and touched them, and the earth felt soft, wet, and perfectly normal. According to the local traditions, they were made some two hundred and fifty years ago, by a holy man of God who habitually preached to all and sundry under this tree. The story runs that one day several " doubting Thomases " in his mixed congregation expressed scepticism concerning his teachings. The good man thereupon remarked that, as a proof that what he was telling them was the truth, the grass would never again grow over the place where he was standing. He then walked away, leaving the marks of his feet under the tree for all of them to see. And, to this day, the grass has not grown over them! It is even said that hay-seed, grass-seed and new turf have been placed there, all to no effect. Everything has died as soon as it was put in—and the footprints remain, a miracle in an age of doubt and disillusion.

We climbed back into the lorry and drove on over the rough road towards Cluanie. I noticed something else I would have liked to stop and examine—a memorial cairn by the side of the road—but I did not like to trouble the driver again. I have since learned that it was erected in honour of one Roderick Mackenzie, an officer who, being tall and fair, allowed himself to be mistaken for Prince Charlie during the hectic days following Culloden, when the Prince himself was in hiding in a cave at Corriedoe, guarded by the " Seven Men of Glen Moriston." Crying " Rascals—would you kill your King? " Mackenzie was slain by the soldiers; and his head was delivered up to the authorities. My informer had no doubt that this heroic ruse facilitated the Prince's escape.

It was raining hard again as we swept into Glen Shiel. The fierce, bare hills were black and grim, rising out of great banks of cloud. Sgùrr nan Spainteach, the first of the Sisters from this end, towered up to what seemed incredible heights against a stormy sky.

Despite the weather, the journey through Glen Shiel was far too fast for my liking. The spell of this dark, mysterious place was upon me again, and I could have stayed for hours watching the great clouds boil and break over the black crests of the hills. I could well believe the local tradition that this glen is haunted by the spirits of those who fell there in 1719. Indeed, if I had stayed there all night, I should have half-expected to hear strange music—the heady, romantic rhythms of old Spain blending with the wild skirl of pipes where Highlander and Latin serenaded the night, each according to his own fashion.

Several other famous men have connections with Glen Shiel. James Hogg, the Ettrick Shepherd, is supposed to have spent a night in a house near the mouth of the glen, on his way over to the Isles— though the date and circumstances of his long journey have now been forgotten. Donnachadh Mór, or Donnachadh Mac Alister (one of the " pretty " sons of a certain Alexander MacRae) was once leading a party of Kintail men through Glen Shiel to join the Jacobite Rising which culminated in the Battle of Sherriffmuir. On the way, they came upon six men struggling to lift a large stone on to a newly-built wall near Achnagart. Duncan told the men to stand aside, lifted the stone himself, and placed it in the required position on the wall. This was the same Duncan whose sword was picked up after his death on the battlefield of Sherriffmuir and is reported to have been exhibited for some years in the Tower of London as " the great Highlander's sword." Another story about this formidable hero tells how he once rescued his mother's foster-brother, Dugald, who was nearly drowned attempting to ford the River Shiel while it was in flood. Thus, Duncan proved himself the stronger man of the two. But Duncan Mór was gentle as well as strong, and it is recorded that on one occasion, when a servant of his father's was taken with fever on the Heights of Cluanie, he took her in his arms, and, disregarding the risk of infection, carried her all the way down to Glen Shiel so that she should have proper attention. The grateful servant-girl afterwards composed a Gaelic song about his kindly act.

The Gaelic poet of Kintail, Ian Mac Mhurachaidh, sings of the happy days spent hunting in Glen Shiel in some of the poems composed after his emigration to America. It is said that his last song was composed while he was a fugitive in the forest following defeat in one of the battles of the War for Independence, during which he fought on the Loyalist side. The following verses of this poem, together with their translations, are taken from the Rev. Alexander MacRae's *History of the Clan MacRae*. After lamenting his plight in the American woods, the poet's heart turns to the far land of Kintail:

> Thoir mo shoraidh le durachd,
> Gus an duthaich 'm bu choir dhomh bhi.
>
> Thoir mo shoraidh Chuitaille
> Am bi manran is oranan.
>
> A'n tric a bha mi mu'n bhuideal
> Mar ri cuideachda sholasach.
>
> Cha be'n dram 'bha mi 'g iarraidh
> Ach na b'fhiach an cuid storaidhean.
>
> Ceud soraidh le durachd
> Gu Sgur-Urain, 's math m' eolas innt'.
>
> 'S tric a bha mi mu'n cuairt di.
> 'G eisdeachd udlaich a cronanaich.
>
> A bheinn ghorm tha ma coinneamh
> Leum bo shoillear a neoineanan.
>
> Sios 'us suas troimh Ghleann-Seile
> 'S tric a leag mi damh crocach ann.
>
> Gheibhte bric air an linne
> Fir ga 'n sireadh 'us leos aca. . .

Take my sincere farewell to the country where I ought to be. Take my farewell to Kintail, the place of mirth and songs. Where I often sat round a bottle with a happy company. It was not the drink I desired but the worth of your stories. A hundred sincere farewells to Scur Ouran, well do I know it. Often was I in its vicinity listening to the bellowing of an old stag. The green mountain opposite to it, bright to me were its daisies. Up and down Glensheil often did I lay an antlered stag low. Trout might be found on the pool, men seeking them with a torch. . .

And at the end:

Tha mi sgith 'n fhogar sa
Tha mi sgith 's mi leam fhein
'S cian bho thir m' eolas mi.

(I am tired of this exile, I am tired in my loneliness, far am I from the land of my acquaintance.)

The poems of Ian Mac Mhurachaidh were brought back to Kintail by his friend, Ian Mac an Gobha, who returned to end his days near Dornie.

Dr. Farquhar MacRae, a descendant of Ian Mac an Gobha (John the Smith's Son), told me many stories of his adventures. He lost an arm in the American War of Independence, and had to return home. He was thereafter known as " fear na leth-laimh," or the one-handed man. He was a simple, truthful man and a beautiful singer. Befriended and sponsored by MacKenzie of Applecross, he eventually succeeded in obtaining a seven years' pension, with interest, from the Government, and was then enabled to rent, with others, the farm of Morvich.

In his old age, after his family had dispersed and his wife had died, he lay dying at Carndu, near Dornie, attended by his grand-daughter, Dr. Farquhar MacRae's mother. One night, he asked his grand-daughter the meaning of all the lights in the room. There was nothing but one candle shining, but she answered quite simply that the angels of the Lord encompass them that fear him. The old man seemed satisfied with her reply, and fell asleep.

At that time, there was an elderly woman living in a bothy by herself on the shore of Loch Duich, opposite the old graveyard. To the first friend who called to see her in the morning, she said: " It's me that heard the beautiful singing going into Clachan Dubhaich last night. Unless I am mistaken, it was the sweet voice of the smith's son." The first arrival from Dornie told of his having died that night. He was buried in the old cemetery, but his grave, alas, is no longer known. Yet, as long as the beautiful poems of his friend live on in Kintail, Ian the Smith's Son will be remembered and venerated as one who helped to perpetuate the beauties of the land of his birth.

CHAPTER VI

THE FALLS OF GLÒMACH

SPRING stretched out her green, cool hands to Summer. The golden sandals of the sun walked on the stream. In my little garden, a lilac-bush burst into fragrant blossom, the great, mauve heads of it tossing in the wind. The scent of its flowers brought back memories of my childhood in the South, when we had a whole colony of lilac-bushes in the apple-orchard, and one could smell their perfume from the garden gate. I remembered how, throughout May and the first week or so of June, our house would be full of the great, heavy clusters—mauve and white and deep purple—so that the haunting fragrance seemed to follow us into every room. The scent of lilac was linked in my mind with all the other wonderful smells of a country childhood—stables, and freshly-cut grass; weedy ponds where we fished for tadpoles; wellington boots, and pink-tipped daisies in the lawn, and the loft where my brother kept his pigeons. For a brief space, I was taken far back into that Never-Never-Land of light and laughter, where everything was new and miraculous, and we stood, without knowing it, at the gates of the City of Gold. . .

Then, the lilac faded and browned; and the rowan took its place. I came back to the present, to the Highlands—and was happy to find a slender, white-blossoming sapling in my own garden. There is a tradition in these hills that the rowan is a powerful charm against the bad fairies; and it was common in the old days for people to hang a branch above the door to ensure added protection. But they tell me that this is no longer done, now that the Old Knowledge has been forgotten. . .

64

There is a similar story about the fir club moss, the Clan MacRae badge which has the power of protecting its wearer from all forms of evil. At one time, the gathering of this plant was accompanied by a special rite to ensure the efficacy of the charm. The moss had to be found by accident, and it was then passed three times with a circular motion in the direction taken by the sun—known in Gaelic as " deasil." During this procedure, the weaver of the spell chanted the following rune:

> Garbhag an t-Sliabh air mo Shiubhal;
> Cha n-eirich domh feud no pudhar.
> Cha mharbh garmaisg, cha dearg inbher mi,
> Cha riab griannisg no glaislig uidhir mi.
>
> (The Fir Club Moss is on my person;
> No harm or mishap can me befall.
> No sprite shall slay me, no arrow shall wound me,
> No fay or dun water-nymph shall tear me.)

The English translation of this ancient rhyme was given to me by Mr. Duncan MacRae of the Dornie Hotel. Far from laughing at the old belief, I have carried a piece of the fir club moss (found by accident) about with me ever since. . .

On a cool, breezy day, I picked some of the newly-opened yellow irises growing outside my little greystone wall. They were hardly more than buds, but blossomed fully in the warmth of my room. I also rescued one or two pheasant-eye narcissi from the rough Apache caresses of the wind. They looked delicate and lovely in a borrowed cut-glass vase, with a few fronds of yellow-green fern out of the crannies of the wall. Their sweet, heady perfume filled the room—and, unlike the lilac, it brought back no memories.

I sat by the window, trying to concentrate on a correspondence course in Gaelic. To aspirate or not to aspirate—that was the question!

FALLS OF GLÒMACH, RIVER GLÒMACH TRIBUTARY OF RIVER ELCHAIG

I remembered a Gaelic speaker remarking that it was easier to learn than German or French, and could only conclude that my brains were getting rusty with age!

The yellow irises stretched up their sharp antennae to the light. The spear-heads of unopened buds lay half-hidden by the delicate curls of fern. The back-curving, paper-white petals of the narcissi had the grace of poised wings. There was no draught in the room, yet they seemed to be trembling on warm breaths of air. Outside, a lamb was bleating mournfully, and I could hear its mother answering lazily and from far away. The sunlight twinkled over shiny blades of grass—and suddenly the old desire swept over me, and my feet ached to be on the road again.

I put aside my books, murmured an apology (in English) to my absent Gaelic-teacher, and went to the kitchen to oil my boots. I had already decided where to go.

And now, to begin this adventure at the beginning. During those first hectic days in Kintail, when I was staying at the hotel and looking feverishly for a house, I made one long and arduous tramp which I have deliberately neglected to describe until now.

It was a still, clear day, with hardly a breath of cloud. Jeannie and I left Dornie early, and set off along the hill-road by the shores of Loch Duich, rejoicing in our youth and strength and the beauty of the morning. I was carrying a vast parcel of sandwiches in my pack, and the binoculars over my shoulder; for we had a day's hard work ahead of us, and would be tramping over completely strange ground.

Away behind us, Loch Alsh swept out and round to the open sea, a curving pathway of silver fire. On the western horizon, the massed crags of the Black Cuillin leaned sombrely against an opal sky. I was able to pick out the great, smooth hump of Marsco—the double-crested knife-edge of Blaven—the sharp cone of Sgùrr Alasdair, towering above his weird brethren in the warm Spring air.

Before us, the road ran away into the blue folds of the nearer hills.

We tramped steadily on through the sunlit morning, at peace with the world. Now we could see the swelling breast of Ciste Dhubh, and the Five Sisters of Kintail gathered round the head of the loch as if looking at their reflections in the water. There was the dark crevasse of Glen Shiel; and there the high curve of the Saddle, pure silver where the sunlight fell on the unmelted snowfields on its crest.

All about us, the yellow whin was setting the braes on fire, and primroses and windflowers raised their pale faces to greet the sun. The young butterwort with its yellow leaves lay like a fallen star in the wet moss by the wayside.

We were tempted to linger at Clachan Duich; but the knowledge of the distance before us drew us on. At Ruarach, we branched off up the rough road to the left, through Lienassie and along a gravel track to the white lodge of Dorusduain. Here, several shaggy collies came bounding out to meet us, but they allowed us to pass after loud barks of greeting and approving tail-wags at Jeannie, who finds the Highland dogs very amiable on the whole.

Our road now plunged into the forest, rising and falling on its way towards the high hills. Before long, green waves of trees closed in on either side, and the incessant music of rushing water broke across the still, pure air. We were now following one of the old " Coffin Roads " along which the men of Kintail used to be brought to Clachan Duich for burial, from as far afield as Glen Strath Farrar. In passing, it might be remarked that the study of these ancient tracks and right-of-ways (in which the West Highlands abound) is a complete subject in itself. There is now an excellent little booklet available, written by the Rev. A. E. Robertson, B.D., Chairman of the Scottish Rights-of-Way Society, and published by the Darien Press of Edinburgh. If you do not emerge from its pages with a desire to follow every one of the tracks and cross-country routes that he describes, then you are not yet completely under the spell of these western hills!

The wind was freshening a little now. Jeannie and I crossed the burn, now tumbling through a deepening gorge, and climbed steadily until we were in an amphitheatre of rolling brown hills, splashed with the new green of the young forests. The surge and splash of countless minor waterfalls was increasing, and silver veins edged with the mauve of birch-trees gleamed on the rough flanks of the mountains.

Soon, the track began to descend, and we again crossed the burn, this time by stepping-stones—a feat at which Jeannie showed a great deal of courage and not much skill! Then the climb began again.

We looked back at the head of the first steep rise, and the whole landscape was shut in by the brown mass of Sgùrr na Mòraich, with the white house of Dorusduain nestling in the hollow. The forest thinned and was lost, and our path meandered through bare, riven hills, away from the music of the stream. Although the sun was still shining, a mixture of rain and snow was drifting down from the east, a cloud of moving silver, burnished by the hard, clear light. We walked on over peat, boulders, and brown heather; and there was no sound anywhere but the far-off crying of gulls flying inland from the sea. Behind and around us, the hills closed in, shutting out the sunlight. A cold wind sweeping along the narrow gulley opening out over the Bealach na Sròine told us that we were approaching the summit plateau.

At last, we surmounted a rise. There, spread out before us, stretching away into dim distance, lay a land of enchantment and desolation, the untouched fastnesses of the high hills. There was the great, snow-streaked mass of Sgùrr nan Ceathreamhnan; and there Màm Sodhail with her head in the clouds, with the white face of Càrn Eige peeping over her shoulder. Behind us, A' Ghlas Bheinn ran up into the massive curve of Beinn Fhada; and away to the north lay Faochag, Aonach Buidhe and the hills guarding the head of Glen Elchaig, of which more later.

In the deep glen below and to our right, the Amhainn Gaorsaic flowed from Loch a' Bhealaich, Loch Gaorsaic and Loch Thuill

Easaich, so that the three pools of water had the appearance of pendants strung on to a silver chain. In passing, we added these to our collection of hill-lochs, as they are set at a height of around 1,242 feet. There was no sign of life around them save a ruined bothy or shooting-lodge and a straggling herd of deer splashing on the fringes of Loch Gaorsaic. Without the glasses, they lay bare and desolate in the bosom of the hills.

We turned away from them, and scrambled down the hillside to our left. Soon, the Amhainn Gaorsaic became a foam-laden torrent, its pace increasing as it ran on over the white rocks. I was listening all the time now for the sound of rushing water, for my map told me that I should be approaching the goal of my long excursion—the famous Falls of Glòmach.

At last, it came—a dull, throbbing roar, echoing and pulsing among the naked hills all around. The stream began to leap and wrestle with itself, hurtling on its hectic way towards the chasm. Then, it leapt two or three steps—and disappeared in clouds of flying foam, falling three hundred and seventy feet into the abyss below.

We followed the path down to the tree, and looked into the gorge. It was dark, thick with wet ferns and loud with the thunder of waters. Far below, among a few sparse silver birches, the tortured stream rushed on out of a great black pool and over huge rocks scarred by primeval fires on its journey through the hills to Glen Elchaig.

I turned away, feeling that if I stayed any longer I should be dazed by the noise and drawn down into the black chasm below.

The Falls of Glòmach are reputed the highest in Britain. The country around them is now National Trust property, having been presented to the Nation by the Hon. G. B. Portman of Inverinate and Mrs. Douglas of Killilan. Sombre, barren, with a wild, distinctive beauty, they are well worth the effort expended in reaching them.

I could not help feeling, as I began the long tramp back to Lienassie, that there must be some stories about Glòmach—and perhaps not altogether pleasant ones! Apart from the fact that the old Coffin Road passes close by, there is a strange " atmosphere " about this wild cataract set amid stark and lonely mountains in the heart of the wilderness.

For several days after my first visit, I prowled around disconsolately, nosing into old history-books and dragging the Falls into conversation with strangers in the hope of getting a " story." In the Rev. Alexander MacRae's valuable *History of the Clan MacRae*, printed in 1899, I found a reference to Dorusduain, in connection with a strange power reputed to have been possessed by some of the natives of Kintail " within very recent times." The story told how Donnachadh nam Piòs, otherwise Duncan of the Silver Cups (compiler and part-author of the celebrated *Fernaig Manuscript*, a collection of the Kintail poetry of the troubled seventeenth century), was one day returning from Glen Affric with his servant. All went well until they reached Dorusduain, where they had to cross the flooded River Conag. The servant, knowing himself to be possessed of the fatal power called " the charm of Friday," which would cause anyone he looked upon in the water to be drowned, went first, and threw himself on his face on the bank so that he would not see his master in the water. He looked up too soon, however, and Duncan was immediately overpowered by the stream. He recovered himself, however, and all would have been well if the servant had not lost all presence of mind and continued to stare, with the result that the noted poet met an untimely death in the torrent!

A few days later, I was told a rather grim tale which would certainly have spoiled my enjoyment of my first visit had I known about it sooner.

A few years ago, the celebrated mountaineer and author, Mr. F. S. Smythe, came up to Kintail, and decided to walk over to Glòmach by the Dorusduain route. At the point where the Bealach na Sròine narrows, he paused for a rest on a little hillock overlooking the glen.

Suddenly, as he sat there absorbing the wild, bare scene, he saw a group of people coming along the old Coffin Road. There were men, women and children, all dirty and very tired. Then, without warning, a crowd of armed men leapt down the hillside and massacred the little group before the horrified eyes of the watcher!

Mr. Smythe tells this strange story in detail in his book, *The Mountain Vision* (published by Messrs. Hodder and Stoughton). My friends at Dornie assured me that this was by no means the first time that queer things had been seen along this road to Glòmach.

Yet another story tells of a man who found a heap of bullets on a hill in the vicinity of the Fall. Thoughtlessly, he sat there picking them up and scattering them in all directions. Several days later, coming back to the same place, he found them all together again, as before. . .

Despite these rather blood-curdling tales, I still maintain that one should visit Glòmach—though I am not sure, now, that I would do it again alone! It is a grand tramp in company, though, and at almost any time of the year (particularly in Spring, when they are in spate, or in Winter, when they are frozen over), the Falls have an unforgettable grandeur.

The main drawback is that, for anyone unaccustomed to hilltramping, they are so inaccessible. From Dornie, there are three routes open to the would-be visitor—the one I have already mentioned, via Lienassie and Dorusduain—and two by way of Killilan. Each way means a day's hard tramping, unless you have a cycle to cover the first stages. Even so, to get there and back again by nightfall is a long and tiring trek of roughly twenty-eight miles, much of it over very uncertain ground. None of the approaches should be attempted without a map. (I was recently told of two ladies who set out, mapless and compassless, for the Falls of Glòmach from Killilan, and ended up in Glen Affric! This would have been more understandable had they been on the Lienassie route, for it is extremely easy to take the wrong track at Dorusduain—in any case, it proves the extent to which one can be misled among the high hills!)

On the first alternative route, I took my cycle and left Jeannie at the cottage, as I was afraid of what mile upon mile of rough gravel road might do to her feet.

It was, as I have said, a cool, breezy day, with the sunlight winking over the blown grasses by the wayside. I pedalled steadily along the shore of Loch Long, with clouds of dust spurting up from my wheels. I remembered to stop at my " road-house " and was given some crowdie—a " cheese " home-made from sour milk, which was to stand me in good stead, later, on the hill.

Through green Glen Elchaig, the wind was very strong and the road going steadily uphill. It seemed that I would never get beyond the big hump of Càrnan Cruineachd, a rocky mass against the travelling clouds. At long last, however, the River Elchaig began to widen a little, flowing more smoothly between big grey stones. Then the beginnings of Loch na Leitreach came into sight, steely blue in the bright light.

I cycled on beyond the stepping-stones to get a look at the head of Glen Elchaig. There, in the distance, was the Iron Lodge, and one or two scattered crofts set against the sunwashed hills beyond. I could see Faochag and the neighbouring peak of Aonach Buidhe, with, in the centre, a steep blue corrie running up to cloud-wreathed An Socach, 3,503 feet.

I went back a little way and had lunch by a large boulder—hard-boiled eggs, rolls, scones, and some of the crowdie, which appealed strongly to my taste.

I then " parked " the dusty cycle, collected my binoculars and the the rest of the food, and crossed the end of Loch na Leitreach by the

THE FERRY HOUSE, TOTAIG

stepping-stones. The water was low, and presented no difficulty. Finding no bridge, I then floundered across the foaming Allt a' Ghlò-maich, and struck up the steep cleft between Càrnan Cruineachd and Meall Scouman. The burn fell away into a deepening gorge below. I lost the rough track, and soon found myself scrambling along the steep face of the gorge, over grey rock and wet, slippery moss, between precariously-balanced silver birches. (I discovered, later, that the real track is much higher up the hillside). Below me, the cliff-face dropped almost sheer to swirling black waters pouring over scorched rock and foaming into great, still pools, dark with depth. I felt as if I were clinging by my eyebrows, and must surely fall. The height, and the incessant roar of rushing water, had a distinctly unnerving effect.

It was a relief to hear a human voice shouting above the wild music of Nature. I scrambled up on to safer ground, and, with the aid of my glasses, picked out a shepherd calling to his dogs on the far hillside. Thereafter, for some reason, I felt safer and a great deal more at home in my surroundings.

I now found a semblance of a path, which descended to cross a burn. Just beyond this point, I became aware of a deep, sinister, familiar throbbing, rising above the rush of the stream. I topped a rise—and there they were again, the grim Falls of Glòmach, roaring down a precipice in the flank of the hill, a vast, cruel torrent pouring into the dark gorge below.

They were rather less majestic from this angle, for I looked up at them, and could not see the complete staircase of the water carving its irresistible way down the grey rock. I climbed one of the hills to my right, and from the summit of this I could see the burn above winding out from the hills, and the little tentative steps it made before it plunged and crashed over the chasm's edge. When I could tear my eyes away from this tumult of foaming waters, I looked back the way I had come, and saw the Allt a' Ghlòmaich frothing and fretting on its way through the green abyss towards Loch na Leitreach.

I descended at last, found the track this time, and was soon through the gorge and cycling homeward again, with a strong following wind.

Once more, it had been a grand day, and it was hard to decide which of these two routes to Glòmach I had enjoyed most. They are in such complete contrast—one, for the most part, a long, steady tramp over peat and heather among bare hills where the silence becomes almost oppressive—the other, a dizzy scramble along the sides of a fierce gorge where, after a while, you would give anything to get the drumming of water out of your ears!

Route number three—also by way of Killilan—is the easiest approach of all, though the path was not marked on my map. Reaching Loch na Leitreach, you go on past the loch to the white house of Carnach, where you cross two bridges and follow a good path up the shoulder of the left-hand hill. This takes you up on to the plateau to a little loch known locally as Loch a' Mhurachaidh, or Murdoch's Loch, linked by a burn to another tiny lochan boasting a picturesque island bearing one dead tree. Passing these, you follow the path to a cairn on which some kind soul has thoughtfully scratched an arrow and the word "Falls." Here, you bear right, and come round the shoulder of Meall Scouman to the Glòmach burn. A short tramp along the side of the rushing water—and you are on the top of the Falls, looking down the whole three hundred and seventy feet into the green abyss, with clouds of foam flying into your face and your knees quivering at the terrific drop.

A short scramble along the flank of Meall Scouman enables you to see the Falls in their rocky setting, with the path winding down to the tree on the other side. Though not so impressive, this unusual view makes the Carnach route well worth while.

My own excursion by way of this third route—also some more legends and traditions about the Falls—receive further discussion in Chapter Fifteen.

CHAPTER VII

MÀM RATTACHAN IN THE RAIN

THE circular walk from Totaig to Glenelg and back over Màm Rattachan is a pleasant, longish tramp, given good conditions. Jeannie and I, however, had the ill-fortune to pick a bad day. It began well enough. We crossed the ferry from Dornie in sunshine and a light, salty wind blowing from the Isles. We did not forget to make an arrangement with the ferryman to take us back at about six o'clock. The ferryman lived at Letterfearn, about a mile from Totaig, and the customary procedure in getting a message to him was to telephone Letterfearn Post Office. They then passed on the message, and the ferryman proceeded to Totaig on his motor-cycle. To avoid delay, therefore, it was advisable to make arrangements in advance—that is, if you are the sort of person who cannot abide delay at any price; or if you have to be back at your hotel in time for dinner.

In my own case, it was the latter consideration which prompted me, this being another trip which Jeannie and I accomplished before we found the cottage at Nostie. Touching the matter of a little delay here and there, I have come to the conclusion that it does not do to be too particular about time in the Highlands. The Highlander will move when he wants to—and not before. And who can blame him? Indeed, after a while, one begins to see a great deal of value in such an outlook, if only as an antidote to the doctrine of rush and clock-watching propagated in the cities. I confess, and quite shamelessly, that I seldom look at my watch, now, in the Highlands. I eat when I want to, sleep when I want to; and if I happen to be in the mood for dreaming away five minutes—what harm ? Who shall say that

75

such dreaming is valueless, when through it one may perhaps reach out to the quiet heart of Nature, and touch hands with the everlasting peace?

Let us dream, then—fine, vigorous dreams of our own. Let us gaze away and away into the blue hills and across the quiet sea, dotted here and there with the faery isles—and let us not be ashamed to admit that what we find there brings us pleasure. And, should our friends reproach us for such introspective meanderings, we can always ask them how many hours they spend each week listening to the radio, or sitting in a cosy cinema, or reading about romances and adventures in the magazine of their choice—and tell them, quite gently and simply, that we prefer to enjoy our dreams in the open air. . .

There is something about the Western Highlands which gets into your blood. If you are a visitor, you will be amazed at the change in yourself after only a few weeks among these lovely hills and glens. You were weary, and tired of life and living? Somehow, you have found rest, and a new outlook. Your nerves were ragged, shattered by the War and the unsettled conditions of the post-War world? Somehow, they are calmed, and your heart is quiet and steady, as if the ghost of some gentle saint had laid his hand on you in passing. You no longer ask passers-by the time, or worry if the butcher does not arrive in time for lunch. Instead, you take sandwiches out on to the sea-shore, and find a dry rock in a nest of sea-pinks, where you sit with your bare feet among a tangle of wet weed, sharing your meal with the gulls. After a while, you will begin to see life through the eyes of the Highlander—and you will understand a great deal that was hidden before.

The scientifically-minded will put this change in you down to the " sea-air " or the " climate "—but you yourself may be secretly aware that it is because you have fallen under the spell of the hills. . .

The walk over Màm Rattachan, as I said, is a pleasant, longish tramp, given good conditions.

From the white house of Totaig, Jeannie and I scrambled up through the woods along the Loch Alsh shore, following a rough path which climbed rapidly from sea-level to a height of 539 feet. Just past the summit, we rested, and gazed down a steep slope of silver birches to the wide reaches of the loch, where the little waves seemed to have been frozen in the very act of motion. The sun was still shining, though less whole-heartedly now. I got out the field-glasses and gazed sea-ward to the white houses and hotels of the Kyle, the little lighthouse, like an ivory tower, on Eilean Bàn, and the ferry to Kyleakin, crawling like a lazy black-beetle across the frosted glass of the sea. I was reminded of the legend about the Norse princess who once occupied the old fort at Kyleakin, now a crumbling ruin. It was said that she had a chain stretched across the narrows between Skye and the mainland, and refused to let any boat pass unless the captain paid her a toll! Even in those far-off days, it seemed, the business of making a living was not confined to the male section of the population.

I put down the glasses, and looked across to Balmacara and Avernish. The little houses seemed lost in a sort of timeless peace, dappled with the moving patterns of sun and shadow. Here and there, a wisp of smoke was rising from a chimney and sailing away on the wind. I searched vainly for the " Prince's Cave " at Balmacara. Actually, there are two caves here which are rumoured to have sheltered " Bonnie Prince Charlie "—one in the rock-face along the shore, and the other high in the cliff near what is known locally as the " Smiddy." Neither, however, was visible from this angle.

I looked back towards Loch Duich. The water was deep blue against the white of the toll-bridge. Eilean Donan Castle, a strange patchwork of old and new stone from this side, watched over the slowly-receding tide. The first curve of Loch Long ran away towards Beinn Dronnaig and the far hills. I could see the red roofs of an occasional byre—among them the one at Nostie, attached to the cottage which, a week or so later, became my summer home. The greystone crofts of Ardelve hugged a shore dark with wet weed.

All around me, the brown hills lay bare to a sky broken by gathering cloud. I remembered a once-common fairytale of Kintail, told to me by Mr. Duncan MacRae of the Dornie Hotel. As the scene of this story is set by the very track over which I was walking, I make bold to retell it here:

During the late seventeenth or early eighteenth century, when the area between Totaig and Glenelg was densely wooded, a MacRae from Ardelve came over to look for a keel for his boat. Now, the important thing, from his point of view, was to find a piece of wood growing exactly the right shape—a task which he judged to be by no means impossible. At first, however, it seemed that the fates were against him. It was a raw day in winter, and soon a thick mist came drifting down the hills. Having wandered off the track, he soon lost his way among the trees. Night fell, and he was still wandering forlornly on the hillside, somewhere between Totaig and Glenelg. He emerged finally from the forest, only to find himself wandering through dense mist and cloud on the open hill, among wet peat and heather which made very hard going.

At last, to his great joy, he saw a light flickering through the mist. Quickening his steps, he came presently to an old shieling, where he halted thankfully and set about making his presence known to the inmates. At his insistent knocking, an old woman came out; but she appeared to be very reluctant to let him in. At last, she consented to allow him to sit beside the fire. Inside the shieling, he found two more elderly women, who shared their companion's disapproval of his intrusion. Finally, however, they gave him a little broth, and he sat on some heather by the fire to dry his clothes. Prompted by some strange instinct, he then pretended to go to sleep. All was silent for a while—then one of the women crept over to him, and the others followed. Having satisfied themselves that he slept, the three old crones went to a chest in the far corner. The first one took out a blue cap, put it on her head, said " Lunnain! "—and promptly disappeared. The second and third did likewise.

At this, the man sprang up in terror and crossed himself. Finally, however, his curiosity overcame his fear of what was obviously witch-craft. Very stealthily, he too went to the chest in the corner, put on a blue cap, and repeated the magic word.

When he came to himself, he was in a large wine-cellar in London— and there were the three witches, very happy indeed! However, as soon as they saw our friend from Ardelve, they put on their blue caps, said " Cinntaille, Cinntaille, air ais! " (Kintail, Kintail, back again!) and vanished like a puff of mountain wind.

Not so, our hero. He, like a true and resourceful Highlander, put his cap into his pocket and settled down to enjoy the good things around him. He was new to the game, however, and the wine-merchants, arriving in the morning, found him in a state which is best described as " incapable." They had been missing wine from this particular cellar for years, and were overjoyed to get their hands on the supposed culprit. The law was harsh towards thieves in those days, and our friend was at once dragged off to the gallows. As was the custom, the hangman asked him if he had any last request to make before he died.

By this time, the fresh morning air had cleared the canny MacRae's head a little, and he solemnly asked permission to put on the blue cap in his pocket and wear it to Eternity. A short consultation was held, and his seemingly harmless request was granted.

No sooner was the cap on his head than he said " Kintail, Kintail, back again! "—and he, the gallows and the hangman all vanished into thin air!

The unfortunate hangman fell off somewhere on the journey; but the hero of our tale came proudly back to Ardelve, and made the gallows (which were exactly the right shape) into the keel for his boat!

Part of this boat is said to be still in the district; but its exact whereabouts have been forgotten now that the old tales are no longer told.

It is of interest to the student of these ancient fairy-tales to note that James Hogg introduces a variation of this same story, in the *Eighth Bard's Song* of the famous *Queen's Wake*. The entire poem is written in medieval Scots, and among the marked differences are that the witches go to Carlisle instead of London, to loot the cellar of a bishop, and the man is to be burned at the stake instead of hanged. This rather leads one to conclude that the story in question was at one time widely known, different districts having their own version of the same tale.

It was beginning to rain as Jeannie and I began our scramble down to Ardintoul. Nothing, however, could have damped my enthusiasm for this delightful little cluster of houses, hugging a shell-strewn shore, backed by the heathery slopes of the hills.

The most outstanding feature of Ardintoul is its colour. We looked down onto red roofs, bright green trees blowing in the wind, the deeper, blue-green of the grass, and golden whin lying like a mantle around the feet of the hills. We crossed the turbulent stream at the foot of a miniature waterfall, where the amber water flowed between high walls of moss-covered rock, among wild irises, primroses and half-opened ferns. Soon we were walking across the machair, on a carpet of short turf dotted with sun-bleached shells, while gulls and oyster-catchers screamed on the fringe of the ebbing tide. Along the pebbly shore, nets were spread over the sea-wall to dry, and the beached boats had a business-like air, as if prepared at any moment to put to sea. The general impression of this little settlement was one of colour, life and industry. Even the geese, emerging in an orderly squad from a farmyard, were full of vigour, and quite prepared to chase us down the road at a word of command from their leader!

We side-stepped this indignity by going quickly of our own accord,

without stopping to argue. Behind the farm, our path branched off, following the crooked telegraph-poles over the hills to Glenelg. Here, we were in open country—and it was at this point that the rain began to come down in earnest.

For the rest of the day, the downpour continued, steadily and without relief. The undulating road ran on and on, until at last, wet and bedraggled, we surmounted the last rise and began the descent to Glenelg Bay.

The isles were shut out by a wall of mist, and our view over the rest of the country suffered likewise. We had only a dim impression of the wide curve of the bay with its houses and imposing hotel. Of Bernera, we could see nothing for walls of driving rain.

It was at Bernera that, in 1722, a barracks was erected in which a few companies of soldiers were usually stationed until after the Battle of Culloden. They were supplied with food and other necessities by sea, for at that time the inland road over Màm Rattachan to Kintail and Glen Shiel was little more than a horse-track. It was greatly improved upon by General Wade, who incorporated it into his military road from Fort Augustus, which ran through Glen Moriston and Glen Shiel and thence over Màm Rattachan to Glenelg. In the nineteenth century the road received further attention at the hands of local work-men, under the direction of the Rev. John MacRae of Knockbain, who had a share at that time in a farm at Ratagan.

It is now a reasonably good track, though towards the summit somewhat rough for cars. I should imagine, however, that the worst way of tackling it is with a cycle, as the climb from either side is long and steep, necessitating a great deal of pushing.

Even walking, there are drawbacks, especially in the rain. Jeannie and I plodded on, past Balavoulin, Scalasaig, and over the five bridges

THE RATAGAN ASCENT.   WADE'S ROADWAY TO GLEN ELG
FROM SHIEL BRIDGE

beyond Achachuirn, with the road rising all the time now on the weary three-mile grind to the summit. Starting from sea-level, you work steadily up to a height of 1,295 feet—and it seems that the brow of the hill will never come! On a clear day, the view would make your efforts worth-while—but in my own case, I was too wet to care! Below, and to my right, wave upon wave of rain-soaked larches rolled downwards to the shining curve of the Glenmore River. Dimly, through the mist, I could see the other road running along the valley, following the curve of the stream. This is another ancient right-of-way long used by the people of the district as a route to Loch Hourn, Glen Garry and over the Bealach Dubh Leac to Glen Shiel. On this particular day, it was only a faint white ribbon threading its way between scattered crofts into the blue curve of the hills.

Before us, the dark skies scowled angrily over the lifting slopes of heather. Rain soaked steadily through my boots and so-called waterproof. Jeannie trotted demurely along at my heels, her long tail trailing in the mud, her coat, with its centre parting, sleeked to her steaming sides. Even wet to the skin and looking as grotesque as something out of a circus, she yet managed to preserve an air of dignity. Perhaps her eyes registered a mute protest beneath her fringe of limp grey hair; but the vigour of her short strides said plainly that if *I* could stick it, so could she.

We reached the summit, and paused for breath in the shelter (?) of some dripping pines. It was at this moment that a welcome roar rose and fell behind us, and a car came bounding up the rough road. Thankfully, we pocketed our pride and accepted a lift. I was sorry for any passenger who might take our place later. It seemed that at least a bucketful of water rolled off us on to the seat and floor of the car!

Soon we could see the great curves and sweeps of the road, twisting and winding down to the rain-shrouded valley.

I thought of Dr. Johnson and Boswell, coming over Màm Rattachan in the opposite direction on Wednesday, September 1st, 1773. I wondered if it had been raining then, for it was reported by the faithful Boswell that Johnson was in a particularly bad humour. Indeed, Màm Rattachan was the scene of what almost amounted to a quarrel between the two weary travellers—though the story is better told in Boswell's own words. After recounting how they had been entertained by members of the Clan MacRae in Glen Shiel, Boswell describes their journey by horse-back to Glenelg:

We rode on well till we came to the high mountain called the Rattakin, by which time both Dr. Johnson and the horses were a good deal fatigued. It is a terrible steep to climb, notwithstanding the road is formed slanting along it; however, we made it out. On the top of it we met Captain Macleod, of Balmenoch (a Dutch officer who had come from Sky), riding with his sword slung across him. He asked, " Is this Mr. Boswell? " which was a proof that we were expected. Going down the hill on the other side was no easy task. As Dr. Johnson was a great weight, the two guides agreed that he should ride the horses alternately. Hay's were the two best, and the Doctor would not ride but upon one or the other of them, a black or a brown; but as Hay complained much after ascending the Rattakin, the Doctor was prevailed with to mount one of Vass's greys. As he rode upon it down hill, it did not go well, and he grumbled; I walked on a little before, but was excessively entertained with the method taken to keep him in good humour. Hay led the horse's head, talking to Dr. Johnson as much as he could, and (having heard him in the forenoon express a pastoral pleasure on seeing the goats browsing) just when the Doctor was uttering his displeasure, the fellow cried with a very Highland accent, " See, such pretty goats! " Then he whistled, whu! and made them jump. Little did he conceive what Dr. Johnson was. . .

What a delicious picture! And how the faithful pen of poor " Bozzy " catches the mood of that harrowing ride! Almost, one can feel the tension in the air, the sense of an impending storm which must have hung over the whole party during that memorable trip. And, of course, it was on the well-meaning Boswell that the mighty wrath was at last vented:

It grew dusky, and we had a very tedious ride for what was called five miles, but I am sure would measure ten. We had no conversation. I was riding forward to the inn at Glenelg, on the shore opposite to Sky, that I might take proper measures before Dr. Johnson, who was now advancing in dreary silence, Hay leading his horse, should arrive. Vass also walked by the side of his horse, and Joseph followed behind, as therefore he was thus attended, and seemed to be in deep meditation, I thought there could be no harm in leaving him for a little while. He called me back with a tremendous shout, and was really in a passion with me for leaving him. I told him my intentions, but he was not satisfied, and said, " Do you know, I should as soon have thought of picking a pocket as doing so."

From here, it seems, things went from bad to worse!

Boswell: " I am diverted with you, sir."
Johnson: " Sir, I could never be diverted with incivility; doing such a thing makes one lose confidence in him who has done it, as one cannot tell what he may do next."

Boswell was, apparently, flabbergasted at all this:

His extraordinary warmth confounded me so much that I justified myself but lamely to him, yet my intentions were not improper. I wished to get on to see how we were to be lodged, and how we were to get a boat—all of which I thought I could best settle myself, without his having any trouble. To apply his great mind to minute particulars is wrong; it is like taking an immense balance, such as is kept on quays for weighing cargoes of ships, to weigh a guinea. I knew I had neat little scales which would do better . . . I, however, continued to ride by him, finding that he wished I should do so.

They came to the inn at Glenelg, where " wretched " conditions were somewhat alleviated by the fact that the factor to the Laird of Macleod sent up a bottle of rum and some sugar. Poor Boswell was still worrying about their near-quarrel; but re-opening the subject brought no consolation:

He was still violent upon that head, and said: " Sir, had you gone on, I was thinking that I should have returned with you to Edinburgh, and then have parted from you, and never spoken to you more."

In the morning, however, the skies had cleared. Johnson owned that he had " spoken in a passion " and chided Boswell for taking him seriously. They had left Màm Rattachan and its trials and tribulations behind, and were on their way to Skye and the Isles.

In passing, it may interest the reader to note that Dr. Johnson's own account of the affair is a great deal more restrained and pedantic —and far less entertaining!

We left Auchnashiels and the Macraes in the afternoon, and in the evening came to Ratiken, a high hill on which a road is cut, but so steep and narrow that it is very difficult. There is now a design of making another way round the bottom. Upon one of the precipices, my horse, weary with the steepness of the rise, staggered a little, and I called in haste to the Highlander to hold him. This was the only moment of my journey in which I thought myself endangered.

Having surmounted the hill at last, we were told that at Glenelg, on the sea-side, we should come to a house of lime and slate and glass. This image of magnificence raised our expectation. At last we came to our inn, weary and peevish, and began to inquire for meat and beds.

Then, having described the difficulties of obtaining food and recounted the episode of the bottle of rum and sugar, the worthy (and distinctly " peevish ") doctor goes on to speak in none-too-complimentary terms of the bed-chamber, where a man " black as Cyclops from the forge " started up from one of the beds at their approach.

Eventually, however, the two weary travellers attained some degree of comfort. The Highlanders brought some hay, and Dr. Johnson slept upon it in his riding-coat. However, " Mr. Boswell, being more delicate, laid himself sheets with hay over and under him, and lay in linen like a gentleman."

In the morning, frayed tempers were calmed and Màm Rattachan was forgotten.

I was not sorry to see the last of it, either. Had it not been for the timely advent of the car, Jeannie might have suffered the same trials as poor Boswell!

The rough road wound on, corkscrewing endlessly (or so it seemed) down to the far gleam of Loch Duich. Then, the long run along the shore beside the grey loch with its white-capped waves and tangle of red and green weed. I noticed a few bedraggled " hoodies " pecking about among the pebbles on the shore, and one or two sleek black-backed gulls; but otherwise the loch was deserted. Ahead, through the mist, we could see the Castle on the far side, looming grey and grim in the rain. All about us, the wet woods tossed in the wind, and the wet, flattened fields sloped up into the unfriendly hills.

Our car took us as far as Letterfearn. There remained only the short tramp to Totaig—and, indeed, we were glad that it was no longer. The rest had made us realise that we were tired, and it was a very bedraggled couple who arrived finally at the ferry.

The tide was now running in fast, and great white-capped waves made a long line of foam across the head of Loch Duich, where the two currents met. While we waited for the ferryman to arrive, a large black fin suddenly broke the surface near the shore. Whatever it was —porpoise or dolphin—it seemed perfectly at home. Three times the fin lifted, moving with a curious rolling motion in the direction of the open sea. Then it was gone, and the loch was empty of life save for a pair of teal which skimmed swiftly across the rain-spattered water.

The ferryman came at last. I apologised for being too early, and we slid down the slippery pier to the boat. Although the tide was nearly in, it had not yet covered the clinging weed, and I, at least, had to pick my steps carefully to preserve my balance and dignity. Jeannie, with four legs, fared a little better; but the expression on her face gave a strong indication of her opinion of sea-weed, boats, rough water and the like as a means of entertainment.

On board I picked her up, and we crouched under the prow together. Remembering that long line of foam out in the middle of the loch, I prepared for the worst.

It was not as bad as I expected. True, the waves came once or twice over the side of the boat, and the force with which we hit the water from time to time seemed designed to split the floor-boards asunder. However, I had fully made up my mind (it being " one of those days ") that we should be drowned—and was therefore agreeably surprised that we were not!

I did not, of course, communicate my fears to the ferryman. Not once during the whole trip had he looked anything but calm, collected, and a trifle bored—an admirable attitude which I outwardly did my best to emulate. Fortunately, neither Jeannie nor myself suffered the crowning indignity of being sick!

On *terra firma* again, and crossing Dornie Bridge, I looked back over our day's excursion. We had seen Màm Rattachan (or some of it), and had made the long circular tramp (or most of it) that we had planned. We had visited Glenelg, and looked across the narrows to the misty shores of Eilean a' Cheò. Perhaps it had not been such a bad day, after all!

And no doubt we would see it all in an entirely new light after a hot bath and a good dinner. . . By to-morrow, I would be telling people how much I had enjoyed it!

CHAPTER VIII

THE LURE OF LOCH DUICH

THE hawthorn was in flower. As I went down each day for my milk, the sweet, strong fragrance accompanied me practically the whole length of the lane. Baby rabbits ran recklessly across the road, and Jeannie chafed at the restraint of the lead. Once, I thought I saw a dormouse, rustling about in the long grass. The weather was hot again, and each day I took my sunbath lying on a raincoat on my wild " lawn."

It was not the whole-hearted heat, though, of a few weeks earlier. Most days, there was a light breeze, and the sky was patched with ragged swirls of cloud. Occasionally, I was awakened early by the sound of raindrops pattering on the windows. On these days, I saw the hills in a variety of moods.

On the day I had planned to make a tramp round Loch Duich, I awoke to find it raining harder than usual. I packed up my lunch and stood at the window, waiting for the weather to clear. Across the road, the hills loomed hazily through blue veils of low cloud. Loch Alsh was grey and unfriendly, ruffled by a passing wind. As I watched, a little boat with red sails came dipping over the small waves, heading towards the open sea. There was a tiny dinghy tied to the stern, and the two of them bobbed slowly past through the mist. The sombre surface of the loch was dappled with a fresh shower of heavy raindrops. On the hills, all colour was subdued to a monotone of dim greens and

ROAD TO LETTERFEARN

blues and greys. The far bleating of sheep added, somehow, to the sadness of the scene. An errant wind bent the wet grasses and sobbed softly in the chimney. Outside, the sparrows chattered crossly, scolding at the weather.

Then, very slowly, as if withdrawn by some unseen hand, the clouds rolled up off the hills. Far vistas of beauty took shape and colour from the awakening sun. The eye was led away into rain-spangled distance, over shining grass and heather bejewelled with a million diamonds, to the proud lift of a distant, sun-washed hill. Gold-dust spattered the grey surface of the loch, where the passing feet of the sun-god brushed and calmed the troubled waters. The twittering of the birds rose to an ecstatic paean of thanksgiving, so that the very air seemed to echo their welcome to returning Beauty.

Jeannie and I went out into a world of warmth and light. The soft morning air was redolent of wet earth and drying grass. The crumpled and battered leaves of the rowan tree were straightening under the caresses of the sun. Somewhere, a cuckoo called triumphantly, mocking the sorrowful croon of the curlew on the shore.

We tramped down to Dornie, and once more crossed the ferry to Totaig. The wet woods seemed to stretch out green arms of welcome, and the gravel crunched delightfully under our feet as we swung along the road to Letterfearn.

From the fringe of this little white village, we had the finest view of the Five Sisters I have yet discovered. They were alive this morning, awake and watchful, the whole five of them rising sharp and distinct against a sky blown clear of cloud. Only in the deep blue gulleys between them, a few frail ribbons of mist yet lingered, like the wraiths of old warriors fighting a losing battle against the encroaching legions of the sun.

We took our time, for there was much to see. Over field, hill and tree, the sunlight had spread her mantle of gold, and a warm wind moved softly all about us, taking fragrance from the rain-soaked pines.

On the shore, the rainbow hues of the shells and pebbles faded to grey and white as they dried under the brilliant sky. Presently, we met some half-Highland cattle, their shaggy coats still plastered to their sides and steaming in the increasing warmth. They did not care for Jeannie, and made this evident. However, they at length condescended to move off the road, and we went blithely on.

The smooth-sloping meadows, refreshed by the downpour, lay like a green patchwork quilt over the knees of the hills. Gulls came down in a cloud of white wings on to brown furrows, or followed the line of a plough. Here and there, the smoke from a grey chimney-stack sailed straight up into the air and was lost on the breeze.

We passed the Youth Hostel at Ratagan, where two bare-footed children played among piles of fresh-cut logs in the yard. They gave me a warm greeting, and laughed at the sight of Jeannie trotting along with her " kilt " swinging and long tail trailing in the dust. Jeannie, who is used to mirthful comments on her appearance, simply flicked one of her tufted ears at them and continued serenely on her way.

We resisted the temptation of Glen Shiel and those hill-lochs up in The Saddle, and continued past the Kintail Lodge and round the head of Loch Duich. We were now at the most desolate part of our journey. The tide was out, and we looked across a mass of peat-waste and weed-entangled shore on which several varieties of gull were dabbling greedily as we passed. At Morvich, so close under the hills that they seemed to press down on us, the desolation increased. It was a relief to get round the bend and on to the grassy cart-track leading down to the churchyard of Clachan Duich, the ancient burial-ground of the men of Kintail.

I opened the iron gate, and we went softly in among the moss-grown stones, some of them leaning over towards each other like old men fallen asleep at their prayers. Of the Church itself, only the four walls are standing, for it was destroyed in 1719, around the same time as the Castle, its Episcopalian vicar being a Jacobite. (The people of

Kintail were for many generations either Episcopalian or Roman Catholic, but a Free Church was built in 1865). Within these crumbling walls of Clachan Duich lie the mortal remains of MacRaes who have achieved fame or become known as leaders among their Clan. There is now a fine memorial-tablet to the MacRaes of Conchra, one panel of which tells, in Gaelic and English, how the Conchra branch of the Clan are direct descendants of Fionnladh Dubh Macgillechriosd, the founder of the Clan in Kintail. It is described how, in 1907, Sir Colin G. MacRae, Writer to the Signet, petitioned the Lord Lyon King of Arms for recognition of his branch as Chieftains of the Clan and for " matriculation in arms." After exhaustive enquiries, however, the petition was refused. Beneath this memorial, executed in red and bronze, appears a replica of the MacRae shield, bearing two stars and a lion rampant, with the motto: *Fortitudine. Nec curo, nec careo.* Also in the ruined Church is a memorial tablet to the same Sir Colin, who was buried in Dean Cemetery, Edinburgh.

The earliest grave with a clear date that I could find was that of " Captain John Stewart, of the Sloop, *Hawke of Rothesay*," accidentally drowned in 1805. Many of the stones, however, are much older, but the writing thereon is no longer legible.

I found the " pleated stone " which marks the grave of a certain Maurice MacRae—Maurice the Generous—who lived around the time of Sherriffmuir. It is lying flat, half-hidden by the broken halves of another stone, by the wall of the ruined Church. The story behind it is well worth the telling.

The said Maurice MacRae, together with his wife, was in the habit of going to Inverness from time to time to buy provisions—as, indeed, was the custom of the Kintail men at that time. One evening, when he and his wife were returning, they stopped for a rest at the Struy Inn. Maurice, being of a friendly disposition, began drinking and " fraternising " with some of the men of Strathglass, with whom there had been intermittent feuds. After repeated efforts to persuade him to continue the homeward journey, his wife lost patience and went on alone, fully expecting that he would catch her up. He did not follow her, however, so she at length became alarmed and hurried home to Kintail. A search-party was organised, but all their efforts to find Maurice were vain. Thereupon, one of the Kintail men disguised himself as a beggar, and went from door to door in Strathglass, hoping to hear news of his missing comrade. One night, while outside the window of a house, he overheard two men talking of the " big white salmon " in a certain pool. In the pool, he found the body of Maurice MacRae. He at once hid it in a safe place, and hastened back to Kintail. The people of Kintail formed a large party and went to bring the body home for burial. On their way back, bearing the luckless Maurice, they passed Comar Churchyard in Strathglass, where it so happened that a funeral was taking place. As the stone was being placed over the grave, the men of Kintail, in the hope of provoking a fight, stepped into the Churchyard and carried it away. However, the Strathglass men, perhaps realising that they were outnumbered, did not make the expected resistance. So the stone was taken all the way to Kintail, carried by relays of willing bearers, and placed over Maurice's grave at Clachan Duich, where it still lies. It is pointed out to the visitor as a " pleated stone," typical of the stones at Comar.

The story goes on to say that Maurice MacRae's grave cannot be used for further burials because the flesh of a murdered man or woman, according to an old tradition, will not decay. In fact, I was assured that the grave has been opened on one or two occasions, and this has been found to be true. Another old belief in the Highlands is that a cock will never crow on the spot where a murder has been committed.

On a little mound overlooking the churchyard is a memorial erected by the Clan MacRae for those lost in the first Great War—a simple figure of a kilted, bare-headed soldier leaning on his rifle, his back against a block of rough granite. Beneath him is a shield bearing a mailed arm wielding the claymore, and the words *Sgur Uran !*

(the Clan MacRae battle-cry), and *Fortitudine*. At the foot of the memorial is carved simply *Gus am bris an là* (Until the day break).

We said goodbye, at last, to this ancient resting-place, leaving the tumbled gravestones and roofless Church looking out serenely across the calm waters. Here and there, a new stone, finely polished and engraved, united the present with the misty past; but the general impression was one of age, and the quiet, resigned beauty which comes only with the passing of many years.

From Clachan Duich, we trudged on over the rise to Inverinate. The rhododendrons were in bloom—big, waxen blossoms of brilliant and exotic hues, in vivid contrast to the dark, shiny leaves. On the gnarled trunk of an old oak-tree, a pair of tree-creepers performed fantastic acrobatics, as if for our especial entertainment. I wondered if this could be one of the oak-trees said to have been brought from France by Duncan of the Silver Cups—though it is an accepted belief now that those ancient trees have been supplanted by younger ones of the same kind.

There is another story about the Gaelic poet which has its setting around Loch Duich. It is said that a strange ship, in passing through Kylerhea, had her mast broken by rough weather. Unable to proceed any further, the captain appealed to Duncan for help. Now, as well as being a distinguished poet, Donnachadh nam Piòs was also a skilled mechanician, and he succeeded in mending the mast so well that the grateful captain gave him a silver herring as a token of his thanks and esteem. It was long an established belief among the people of Kintail that Duncan's silver herring was possessed of strange powers, and had a magnetic attraction for the real herring which it could draw in great shoals into Loch Duich, to the undoubted benefit of the Kintail fishermen.

It was Duncan's poetry, however, and his work in connection with the important *Fernaig Manuscript*, which brought him his greatest fame This notable collection of Jacobite and Episcopal poetry—the greater part of which is believed to have been composed by Duncan himself—is judged by many to be next to the *Dean of Lismore's Book* in importance to the student of Gaelic literature. It is also of great value to the historian, in that it gives a clear picture of the religious and political leanings of the men of Kintail during the Revolution.

Another Duncan whose name is remembered in connection with Loch Duich and Inverinate is the celebrated Duncan Mór Mac Alister, some of whose exploits have been discussed in an earlier chapter. It is said that when this Duncan was a young man, he lived for some time on the Letterfearn side of Loch Duich, and used to swim across the loch regularly to visit his sweetheart at Inverinate. On one occasion he is reported to have met a savage Highland bull about half-way across —but to a man of his strength and talents such an untoward happening might be turned from a menace to an advantage. And such, indeed, proved to be the case. Twisting about in the water, Duncan managed to grasp the bull (literally) by the horns, and swing himself up on to its back. He then compelled the bewildered animal to swim across with him the remainder of the distance to Inverinate!

Beyond Inverinate, the road runs sharply up the brae towards Keppoch. The sun blazed down on us as Jeannie and I tramped along. I could feel the warmth of the road through my shoes, and was soon out of breath with the climb.

We rested at the bridge over An Leth Allt, gazing down at the foaming burn as it rushed over white rocks. I had been told that this part of the road is said to be haunted by the ghost of a black dog which can occasionally be seen running across the road. However, we did not see it that day, and I could only conclude that the brilliant sunlight was a discouragement to such strenuous activity, and that the weary ghost was lazing with its tongue out somewhere up the hillside.

At last, we were at the summit of the brae. Below us, the whole wide and lovely expanse of Loch Duich flashed and winked in the sunshine, streaked with dark shadows near the edges, where the hills looked at themselves in the clear water. A grey heron flew with slow, heavy wing-beats along the near shore. High on the hills above blue Glen Shiel, the heat-haze was shimmering like a mirage in the sand-dunes of some far desert. Away to the west, the silver waters swept in a wide curve past the white house of Totaig and away up Loch Alsh to the open sea. Beyond, on the misty horizon, the "far Cuillins" watched over the golden "road to the Isles." It needed no very great imagination to transport the mind back to the days of the Lord-ships, or even farther into the mists of time, when the marauding galleys of the fair-haired Norsemen sailed up this same loch, to the accompaniment of strange songs and the sound of many oars.

Indeed, I thought, Loch Duich has seen many wild and wonderful things, many generations of men come and go across the changeless face of her waters. Her very name is an echo of far-off days, when St. Duthac preached the new Gospel of the Brotherhood of Man among the wild warriors of this fair and bloodstained land. Although this Irish saint later moved to Tain, following the death of his friend, Carrac, his name has a prominent place in Kintail legend and tradition, and the old Church of Kilduich was dedicated to him as a lasting memorial to his work.

Loch Duich is Duthac's Loch—Kintail a simplified version of Cinn-t-Sàile, or the Head of the Salt Water, a name no doubt derived from its being centred around the meeting-place of Loch Duich, Loch Alsh and Loch Long. Many are the tales which are still told about the "old days," before the restoration of Eilean Donan Castle and, more recently, before the building of the new bridge* at Dornie. From the rather wistful talk of some of the older inhabitants, one would gather that they preferred things as they were, with the Castle a picturesque and crumbling ruin, covered with the kindly ivy and haunted by birds of passage from the sea. Yet, they will admit that the changes have been in many ways of benefit to those faced with the

* The toll was removed from the bridge in 1946, during my visit.

arduous business of making a living in the Highlands—though, in the case of the bridge, opinions differ again. Some will say that it was better when the cars would be queueing on each side of Loch Long, waiting for the ferry, for then the hotels and local cottages did a roaring trade in luncheons, teas, and even bed-and-breakfast. Now, it is complained, the cars go straight through, all making for Skye—which is a pity, for they do not know what they are missing if they ignore Kintail! Though I would be the last person to discredit the wild glories of Eilean a' Cheò, I cannot but feel that, in a gentler mood, Kintail, Glen Shiel and Loch Alsh have as much, if not more, to offer to the seeker after beauty. Where, in all the Western Highlands, could the poet or painter find greater inspiration than in sombre Glen Shiel, with its air of romance and " the print of olden wars." And where will the weary traveller find deeper solace for his tired heart than along the shores of blue Loch Duich, where the great hills lie clustered about the quiet waters, and sea-birds call softly to each other in the dusk?

As I said, there are two schools of thought touching the matter of the bridge at Dornie. People who consider it an advantage will tell many tales of the difficulties during the days of the ferry, when strong currents periodically swept the big motor-ferry off its course and carried it quite a distance up Loch Long, while streams of cars were waiting on each side. Indeed, when the tide is running in, one can well understand how this would have happened. Sometimes, at evening, I have fished from the bridge; and the surging current sweeping round the stone pillars has made me quite dizzy. Incidentally, for the benefit of would-be anglers, I might remark that the fishing from Dornie Bridge well repays investigation. Under the right conditions—preferably at evening, with a fast in-coming tide—one can land quite a good haul of " cuddies " and a big yellowish fish called lithe with which to supplement the rations. Both are extremely good eating, if cleaned and cooked as soon as possible. The lithe,

particularly, taste pleasantly of the sea—and one of these is usually enough for three people. The usual bait used is a rubber eel or one of those brightly-coloured metal minnows, so that there is none of the disagreeable business of baiting hooks—an important asset, from my point of view!

The less energetic among us will find sufficient entertainment in just standing quietly on the bridge, watching the light change and change again across the waters of Loch Duich as the sun sinks behind the western hills. For my own part, there are evenings when to fish or do anything at all would be in the nature of a sacrilege; for Kintail upon occasion produces a sunset that beggars description. Only a prose-writer like Maurice Walsh, a poet like Stevenson, or a painter like Finlay Mackinnon could begin to express, on paper, the trans-formation of earth, sea and sky under the gentle hands of the Great Artist.

Such a sunset it was my privilege to witness on the particular evening when Jeannie and I returned to Dornie after our sixteen-mile tramp around Loch Duich.

The tide was at the full, and the waters of the quiet loch were a soft, sleek grey, with pink understones shining through, as if reflected from coral caverns far beneath. The sky was a cool, translucent blue, splashed here and there with whorls and streaks of mauve and orange, like an artist's palette on which the colours had been tried out before use. All over the vast arch of the heavens there were great spirals of smoky grey, and feathery stipplings of delicate green, with rows of mauve dapples in between—all assuming the oddest shapes and producing the most varied of effects. As the sun sank lower, and the flame began to flicker and die beyond the western horizon, so the sky faded slowly to a quiet, transparent grey, devoid of colour save where patches of

THE GLEN SHIEL HILLS AND THE WOODED SLOPES AT KEPPOCH

faintest rose traced a path beyond the hills, as if a fairy had recently passed that way, leaving the prints of her pink feet among the heavenly isles.

Above the Cuillin, turrets of pale mauve cloud added queer crags and precipices to the fantastic outline of the hills, until one could scarce tell the jagged rock from the misty pinnacles of vapour hanging stationary in a windless sky.

All too soon, the last spark of sunglow went out behind the islands, and sky and sea met in an indistinguishable line of far-away blue. Around the dark mirror of the loch, the whole landscape lay grey and still, and the vast upsurge of the shadows had blown out the golden lamps of the whins and shut away the reflections of the coral caves in the depths of the sea.

It was as if the Artist, growing tired, had thrown a dust-sheet over his masterpiece, and mixed all the colours on his palette to a monotone of lifeless grey—with only here and there a wisp of forgotten gold to bring back remembrance of strange beauty.

CHAPTER IX

SEERS AND SAYINGS

IT is impossible to live for long in the Highlands without coming into contact with that mysterious phenomenon known as the " Second Sight." Kintail, in particular, seems rich in tales and traditions of the occult, for it lies in the midst of a district made famous by Coinneach Odhar, or Dun Kenneth, the celebrated " Brahan Seer," whose prophecies have been proved by history to have an often unfortunate habit of coming true!

Most of these prophecies were made between the years 1630 and 1679, and accounts vary as to how Coinneach Odhar obtained his mystical powers of foretelling the future. He is thought to have been born at Uig, in the Isle of Lewis; and one well-known story tells how his mother, while tending cattle one day near a churchyard, saw the graves open and the spirits of the dead going away in all directions. She waited until they returned, and then placed her distaff across the grave of a tall and imposing lady, refusing to let her in until she had recounted where she had been. The ghost said she had visited Norway, and gave Kenneth's mother a stone as a reward for her courage. This stone came into the possession of Kenneth, and from that moment he was enabled to read the future.

Another story tells how, while Kenneth was cutting peats, he fell asleep waiting for his wife to bring his dinner out on to the moor. When he awakened, he found a small blue stone, with a hole in the middle, under his head. He picked it up—and immediately had a vision of his wife coming with the dinner, and could even see of what the meal consisted.

Yet a third version describes how, while serving as a labourer to a wealthy clansman near Brahan Castle, he became very unpopular with his employer's wife, who resolved to poison him. Finding him lying asleep, she set down the poisoned food beside him and went away. When he awoke, he was prevented from eating by something pressing against his heart, and found a beautiful stone like a pearl. As he gazed at it, he suddenly found that he was looking into the future, seeing not only men's actions, but the motives and plots behind them. From that day, he prophesied many startling events, some of which have yet to come to pass. Finally, he was burnt at the orders of the Countess of Seaforth, for revealing that the Earl, who was away on the Continent, had found a new mistress and all but forgotten his unfortunate wife.

It was while he was being led to execution that Kenneth delivered his famous prophecy on *The Doom of the House of Kintail*:

. . . I see a Chief, the last of his House, both deaf and dumb. He will be the father of four fair sons, all of whom he shall follow to the tomb. He will live careworn, and die mourning, knowing that the honours of his line are to be extinguished for ever, and that no future Chief of the Mackenzies shall bear rule at Brahan or in Kintail. After lamenting over the last and most promising of his sons, he himself shall sink into the grave, and the remnant of his possessions shall be inherited by a white-coifed lassie from the East, and she is to kill her sister. And as a sign by which it may be known that these things are coming to pass, there shall be four great lairds in the days of the last deaf and dumb Seaforth (Gairloch, Chisholm, Grant and Raasay), one of whom shall be buck-toothed, another hare-lipped, another half-witted, and the fourth a stammerer Chiefs distinguished by these personal marks shall be the allies and neighbours of the last Seaforth; and when he looks round and sees them, he may know that his sons are doomed to death, that his broad lands shall pass away to the stranger, and that his race shall come to an end.*

The story of the fulfilment of this prophecy has been told many times, and it is agreed by all who have studied the history of the House of Seaforth following the troubled days of the Jacobite risings that Coinneach Odhar's words were in every particular accurate. Francis,

* The prophecies included in this chapter are quoted from *The Prophecies of the Brahan Seer*, by Alexander Mackenzie, F.S.A. Scot., by permission of Messrs. Eneas Mackay, Stirling.

Lord Seaforth, the last Baron of Kintail, though an upright and honourable man, fought in vain against the evil star that marked his destiny. He was compelled, as a result of financial embarrassments abroad, to sell part of his Kintail estates—this despite the fact that his clansmen did their utmost to prevent the lands passing out of the family. About this time, his only remaining son died; and, in January 1815, the broken-hearted father himself passed on, so that:

> Of the line of Fitzgerald remained not a male
> To bear the proud name of the Chiefs of Kintail.

All the circumstances preceding his death had been as prophesied by the Brahan Seer—the four great contemporary lairds with their peculiar physical marks—the untimely death of Seaforth's sons—and Seaforth himself, who was deaf and had formerly been dumb.

What was left of the estates then passed to the young widow of Admiral Sir Samuel Hood—the " white coifed (or white-hooded) lassie from the East "—who, while driving a pony carriage in the woods near Brahan Castle with her sister, was involved in an accident in which the sister was killed. Thus, the prophecy, which had been current for generations in the Highlands, was accomplished to the letter.

It is interesting to note that Dr. Johnson, during his Highland Tour, evinced an open-minded attitude on the subject of the Second Sight. While he and Boswell were at Broadford, in Skye, he made enquiries of a minister, Mr. Macpherson, concerning its reputed existence. On being told that it was not to be believed in because founded on no principle, the worthy Doctor gave a surprisingly unbiassed and un-Johnsonian reply:

There are many things, then, which we are sure are true, that you will not believe. What principle is there, why a loadstone attracts iron? Why an egg produces a chicken by heat? Why a tree grows upwards, when the natural tendency of all things is downwards? Sir, it depends upon the degree of evidence that you have.

In his *Journey to the Western Islands of Scotland*, Dr. Johnson further defines the Second Sight in an attempt to get at the root of the mystery:

" Second Sight " is an impression made either by the mind upon the eye, or by the eye upon the mind, by which things distant or future are perceived, and seen as if they were present. A man on a journey far from home falls from his horse; another, who is perhaps at work about the house, sees him bleeding on the ground, commonly with a landscape of the place where the accident befalls him. Another seer, driving home his cattle, or wandering in idleness, or musing in the sunshine, is suddenly surprised by the appearance of a bridal ceremony, or funeral procession, and counts the mourners or attendants, of whom, if he knows them, he relates the names, if he knows them not, he can describe the dresses. Things distant are seen at the instant when they happen. Of things future I know not that there is any rule for determining the time between the sight and the event. . .

I do not find it to be true, as it is reported, that to the second sight nothing is presented but phantoms of evil. Good seems to have the same proportion in these visionary schemes as it obtains in real life: almost all remarkable events have evil for their basis; and are either miseries incurred, or miseries escaped. Our sense is so much stronger of what we suffer, than of what we enjoy, that the ideas of pain predominate in almost every mind. What is recollection but a revival of vexations, or history but a record of wars, treasons and calamities? Death, which is considered as the greatest evil, happens to all. The greatest good, be it what it will, is the lot but of a part.

That they should often see death is to be expected; because death is an event frequent and important. But they see likewise more pleasing incidents. A gentleman told me, that when he had once gone far from his own island, one of his labouring servants predicted his return, and described the livery of his attendant, which he had never worn at home; and which had been, without any previous design, occcasionally given him. Our desire for information was keen, and our inquiry frequent. Mr. Boswell's frankness and gaiety made everybody communicative; and we heard many tales of these airy shows, with more or less evidence and distinctness. . .

After the two travellers had returned to Edinburgh, Boswell gives, without his characteristic flippancy, his own considered opinion:

October 16.—I beg leave now to say something upon Second Sight, of which I have related two instances, as they impressed my mind at the time. I own, I returned from the Hebrides with a considerable degree of faith in the many stories of that kind which I heard with a too easy acquiescence, without any close examination of the evidence; but, since that time, my belief in those stories has been much weakened, by reflecting on the careless inaccuracy of narrative in common matters, from which we may certainly conclude that there may be the same in what is more extraordinary. It is but just, however, to add, that the belief in Second-Sight is not peculiar to the Highlands and Isles. . .

And neither, continues Boswell, can a belief in Second-Sight be imputed altogether to superstition:

To entertain a visionary notion that one sees a distant or future event may be called superstition; but the correspondence of the fact or event with such an impression on the fancy . . . has no more connection with superstition than magnetism or electricity.

Another celebrated diarist, Samuel Pepys, discusses the phenomenon at length in his correspondence with Lord Reay of Durness, Dr. Hickes and the Earl of Clarendon. Pepys comes to much the same conclusion as Johnson and Boswell concerning the advisability of keeping an open mind.

During my memorable summer among the hills and glens of Kintail, I had the good fortune to meet several Highlanders who believed firmly in the subject under discussion—and one old man who rather suspected himself to have inherited the gift of Second Sight from his mother. I spent an afternoon sitting by his fireside, while he poured out to me tale after tale in support of his convictions, interspersing his stories with picturesque phrases of Gaelic, shaking his head sadly over the disbelief of modern youth. In the same room with us sat a lady and gentleman—the lady eighth in descent from the ill-fated Maurice MacRae who was murdered in Strath Glass. She, too, had many fascinating tales to add about knocks on the window and the sound of a coach drawing up in the dead of night when no coach was there. I learned how, at one time, the key to the churchyard was kept in this very house, and how the mistress (the mother of the story-teller) would hear the spades rattling on the shelf when someone was coming to dig a grave. There were stories of murders and suicides, all heralded or revealed later by the mysterious signs visible only to those who have "The Gift." Most vivid of all was my host's story of how, one evening, he had called the attention of the company to a light in his inside pocket—that pocket into which, a few days later, he had unthinkingly placed the pall-cloth for a dead child's coffin. Then he went on to tell me how he had seen a phantom funeral on the road from Loch Hourn to Tomdoun, and had at first mistaken the carriages for coal-carts which were working near Loch Hourn at the time—until they disappeared, at the point where the real funeral-procession turned off the road a few days later. . .

From the realm of the occult, the conversation then ran on to local history, and I learned how Avernish was thought to have once been an island, with the sea flowing over what is now the main street on the flatlands of Balmacara. Although my host did not exactly *say* it, I got the feeling that he believed that one day the sea would come back to claim its own. He described how, no matter where you dig in this vicinity, you come to sand, white shells and clean, sea-bleached stones —and how once, in 1882, he himself had " met the sea " when he went down to tend the cattle after a storm. After receding, the tide had come back in to sweep the streets, washing up boats into the fields, breaking down sheds and scattering debris in all directions over the ravaged land. There had been a rush to lead the cattle to safety—and, after a while, very slowly, the greedy waters had gone down again, flowing back into the grey wastes of Loch Alsh, to rest in uneasy slumber until they should re-awaken to reclaim the unprotected land.

Needless to say, I returned to the cottage at Nostie with a mind that was far from easy—and subsequent delvings into historical works and fuller accounts of Highland psychic phenomena did not help to set it at rest!

I learned of one of Coinneach Odhar's as yet unfulfilled prophecies concerning the MacRaes of Kintail, who, it is said, would have a deadly encounter with the Maclennans over a squint-eyed tailor. After the battle, the remnant of the MacRae clan would be shipped to Ireland, and the Maclennans would take over their lands.

All this, it was prophesied, would be preceded by a quarrel over a funeral in Kilduich churchyard, originated by the Macmillans. One authority reports that the quarrel has already happened—but the rest of the prophecy is yet to come.

Also, concerning Kintail:

The day will come when the jaw-bone of the big sheep will put the plough on the rafters; when sheep shall become so numerous that the bleating of the one shall be heard by the other from Conchra in Lochalsh to Bun-da-Loch in Kintail, they shall be at their height in price, and henceforth will go back and deteriorate, until they disappear altogether, and be so thoroughly forgotten that a man finding the jaw-bone of a sheep in a cairn, will not recognise it, or be able to tell what animal it belonged to. . .

(Judging from the fine herds at the Conchra Sheep-Dog Trials recently, this prophecy is not likely to be fulfilled for some years to come!)

But, according to the Brahan Seer, there will come a day when:

The ancient proprietors of the soil shall give place to strange merchant proprietors, and the whole Highlands become one huge deer forest; the whole country will be so utterly desolated and depopulated that the crow of a cock shall not be heard north of Druim-Uachdair; the people will emigrate to islands now unknown, but which shall yet be discovered in the boundless oceans, after which the deer and other wild animals in the huge wilderness shall be exterminated and drowned by horrid black rains. The people will then return and take undisturbed possession of the lands of their ancestors.

Some of this, of course, has in part been fulfilled; but, if we are to take it as literally as it is possible to take most of Coinneach Odhar's prophecies, there is still worse to come!

There is another fearsome prediction concerning a battle which will be fought some day at Ardelve, " when the slaughter will be so great that people can cross the ferry over dead men's bodies." We can only hope that Dornie Ferry, and not Totaig, is the one referred to, and that the bridge will be instrumental in modifying the destruction!

Far be it from me, however, to take sides on such a controversial subject as that of the Second Sight. There is so much to be said for and against that, like Johnson, Boswell, Pepys, and many others, I shall continue to keep an open mind.

After all, one cannot live in the Highlands for any length of time without absorbing some of the atmosphere of wild places—without being made aware that " there are more things in Heaven and Earth. . ."

All this leads us naturally to a ghost-story about a glen on which I have so far written very little—Glen Lichd, at the back of the Five Sisters, the scene of the celebrated Glenlic Hunt, famous in the legends and traditions of Kintail. If for no other reason than that it inspired some notable poetry among local bards, this strange episode is well worth recounting.

Glen Lichd was known of old as one of the three great glens of Kintail. It is still thought by many to be haunted as the result of a mysterious murder which occurred there during the seventeenth century. Indeed, one or two old people go so far as to say that foot-prints have been seen there when the snow is lying on the ground—the impression of a three-toed foot with long claws, which is too large to belong to any known creature.

At the time at which the murder took place, a party of young men were out in Glen Lichd on a hunting expedition. For no apparent reason, one of their number, a certain Murdoch, disappeared without trace. For fifteen days and nights the party searched for their lost companion, and while the search was going on, several notable elegies were composed describing his fine qualities and the grief of his young wife at his presumed death. Some of these poems were thought to have been composed by Murdoch's brother, Duncan—others by the celebrated Lochaber bard, Ian Lom.

Finally, on the fifteenth day, the body was found at the foot of some crags—but there were no signs to show the manner of his death.

From this, the tradition grew that the glen was haunted by a mysterious monster—and, many years later, a man set out to break the spell.

Armed with two pistols loaded with silver bullets, he sat in the glen for fifteen days and nights, watching over the place of Murdoch's death. Nothing happened—but on the sixteenth day he returned home, very depressed and shaken, and would say nothing except that he had been unable to exorcise the evil spirit.

And so the legend grew—and the elegies on the unfortunate young man were added to the literature of Kintail.

And, indeed, Glen Lichd is a place well suited by Nature as the abode of evil spirits. Grim, dark and forbidding, the great hills over-shadow it at every turn. Massive Beinn Fhada, with its black serrated edge looming against grey cloud. The austere Sisters blocking out the cold green light flowing inland from the sea. The long, gloomy ridge of Sgùrr a' Bhealaich Dheirg (The Peak of the Red Pass) keeping watch over the climbing path at the head of the glen. The lonely cottages tucked away in a strip of wet meadowland at the foot of the dark hills. Even a "human interest" story about an old man of the glen who entertained a young student from Aberdeen to supper, and lit the fire with *whisky*, does little to lighten the atmosphere of fore-boding which hangs over Glen Lichd like a pall on all but the sunniest days.

Somehow, we cannot escape from the knowledge that a man met his death here—and it is still unexplained.

LAMENT FOR MURDOCH MACRAE OF INVERINATE, KILLED IN THE GLENLIC HUNT.

'S i sealg Geamhraidh Ghlinne-Lic
A dh' fhag greann oirnn tric a's gruaim,
Mu'n òg nach robh teann 'sa bha glic,
'S an' teampull fo'n lic 's an' uaigh.

A' cheud Aoine na Gheamhradh fhuar,
'S daor a phaigh sinn buaidh na sealg,
An t-òg bu chraobhaiche snuagh,
Na aonar uainn a's fhaotainn marbh.

Tional na sgìre gu leir,
Ri siubhal sleibh, 's ri falbh bheann,
Fad sgìos nan coig latha deug,
'S am fear dìreach treun air chall.

Murchadh donn-gheal mo rùn,
Bu mhìn-sùil 's bu leannan mnàoidh,
A' ghnuis anns an robh am ball-seirc,
'S a bha tearc air thapadh làimh.

Chuala mise clarsach theud,
Fiodhall a's beus ag co-sheinn—
Cha chualá a's cha chluinn gu brath,
Ceol na b'fhearr na do bheul binn.

Bu tu marbhaich' 'bhalla-bhric bhàin,
Le morbh caol, fada, geur;
Le cuilbheir bhristeadh tu cnaimh,
'S gu'm bu shilteach fo d' làimh na féidh!

'Bhean uasal a thug dhuit gaol,
Nach bi chaoidh na h-uaigneas slan,
'S truagh le mo chluasan a gaoir,
Luaithead 's a sgaoil an t-aog an snàim.

Gur tuirseach do gheala bhean òg,
'S i 'sileadh nan deoir le gruaidh,
'S a' spionadh a fuilt le deòin,
'Sior chumha nach beo do shnuagh.

'S tursach do chinneadh mor deas
Ga d' shireadh an ear 's an iar,
'S an t-òg a b'fhiùghantaich beachd
Ri slios glinne marbh 's an t-sliabh.

Tha Crathaich nam buailtean bò
Air an sgaradh ro-mhòr mu d' eug—
Do thoir as a bheàtha so òg
A ghaisgich nan corn 's nan ceud.

'S tùirseach do sheachd braithrean graidh,
Am pearson gu h-ard a leugh,
Thug e, ge tuigseach a' cheird,
Aona bharr-tuirs' air cach gu leir.

Bho thùs dhiubh Donnchadh nam pìos,
Gillecriosd, a's dithis do'n chléir,
Fearchar agus Ailean Donn,
Uisdean a bha trom na d' dhéigh.

'S math am fear-rannsachaidh an t-aog,
'Se 'm maor e a dh-iarras gu mion;
Bheir e leis an t-òg gun ghiamh,
'S fàgaidh e 'm fear liath ro shean.

This lament is taken, with the Society's permission, from *The Transactions of the Gaelic Society of Inverness* (*Vol. VIII.*), *Leaves from my Celtic Portfolio*, by Mr. William Mackenzie. The author is unknown. The English translation is given as follows:

The winter hunt in Glenlic has made us often shudder in our sadness about the youth who was not parsimonious, yet was prudent, now lying in a grave under a stone in the temple. The first Friday of the cold winter dearly did we pay for the success of our hunt—the young man of most comely appearance alone was missing, and to be found dead. All the people of the parish searching on moor and mountain during the weariness of fifteen days, for the athletic brave man who was missing. The fair complexioned Murdoch of my choice, of gentle eye, the beloved of woman, of a countenance with the expression of kindness, and rare for prowess of arm. I have heard the stringed harp and the violin in harmony playing with it, I have neither heard, nor shall ever hear sweeter music than (the converse of) thy melodious mouth. Thou couldst kill speckled white trout, with long straight and sharp spear; thou couldst break bones with the gun, and the deer bled freely at your hand. The gentle woman who gave thee her love, and who can never be well in her solitude— it pains my ears to hear her lamenting how soon the marriage knot has been undone by thy death. Sad is thy gentle young wife, with tears flowing down her cheek, plucking her hair with her hand in bitter grief that there is no longer any life in thy countenance. Sad was thy great and accomplished clan, searching for thee east and west, while the youth of most sympathetic judgment was (dead) on the moor on the side of the glen. The Macraes of the cattle folds are grievously afflicted by thy death—taken out of life so young, thou generous hero of becoming conduct. Sad are thy seven beloved brothers—the parson, though profound is his learning, though his office is one of giving comfort, yet he surpassed the others in his grief. First among them is Duncan of the Silver Cups, then Christopher and the two clergymen, Farquhar, Allan of the auburn hair, and Hugh, who was sad after thee. Death is an excellent searcher, a messenger who chooses in a special way, he removes the unblemished young man, and leaves the grey-haired and very old man.

CHAPTER X

THE IRON LODGE

I T was at about this time that I began to feel the need of new inspiration. The last of the Spring flowers had browned and died, and the long, lush hayfields were ripe for the cutting. Nature seemed to be standing still—pausing, as it were, before making her next gesture to Creation.

I forsook the hills for a while, and began to read. I read Alexander Smith's *Summer in Skye*; Swinburne; Fiona MacLeod. Anew, I found time to wonder that the last appears so seldom in anthologies. Perhaps such poetry is no longer fashionable. We are too hard-headed, now, to find the " Immortal Hour " . . .

Or are we ? I read hungrily, the answer eluding me:

> Deirdre the beautiful is dead . . . is dead!
> The grey wind weeps, the grey wind weeps, the grey wind weeps:
> Dust on her breast, dust on her eyes, the grey wind weeps!
> Cold, cold it is under the brown sod, and cold under the grey grass:
> Here only the wet wind and the flittermice and the plovers pass. . .

I thought of possible criticisms which could be levelled against such writing. " Ivory tower " poetry. Romantic. Exaggerated. Remote from the needs and sophistications of Twentieth Century life. Lacking in " social significance." Introspective and out of touch with " modern trends of thought " and " the needs of the New World."

I read on: I turned over the pages to *The Hour of Beauty*:

> Beauty, sad face of Beauty, Mystery, Wonder,
> What are these dreams to foolish, babbling men?—
> Who cry with little noises 'neath the thunder

Of ages ground to sand,
To a little sand.*

Escapist? Perhaps. And yet—was the Earth really so different, after all? When we had broken all the spells, and driven the fairies out of their grassy knolls, was there not still, on the wind, a hint of laughter, where Dalua, the Fairy Fool, mocked us from " the vast gulf of dreadful silence and the unpathwayed dark "? . .

Let me say, at once, that I believe in the New World we are trying to build together. The sorrows, the inequalities, the barbarities of the old have had their day, and few will lament their passing. I believe in the Brotherhood of Man, and a world unshadowed by the threat of War. I believe that health and happiness are the right of the whole community and not the privilege of the few. But I do not think we shall ever build a sane or lasting material world if we ignore the world of the spirit. The very reaching towards beauty is in itself a spiritual quality, and it is a man's capacity for loving, for under-standing, for sharing the hopes and fears of his fellows (all attributes of the spirit) which spur him on to the practical realisation of his dreams. The answer, when we find it, must have its roots in Love.

So I am not really afraid that romance and beauty are being strangled to death by twentieth-century materialism. I might even go so far as to say that I believe we are on the verge of a great re-awakening—a new Renaissance which will unite a growing sense of responsibility for the material comfort of our brothers of all races and creeds with a new and fuller understanding of " the windy headlands of the soul, the lone sands of the mind."

In that World, there may yet be a place for " The joyous Shee, old gods, all beautiful words, Song, music, dreams, desires " that " sway like blown moths against the rosewhite flame. . ." For, however

* These two verses from the *Poems and Dramas* of William Sharp (Fiona MacLeod) are quoted by permission of Mr. Noel F. Sharp, his Literary Executor.

hard-headed we may think ourselves to be, we shall never be content with half-a-world!

It was raining as I closed the book. Cycling down to the farm for my milk, I saw two rainbows in the sky at once, a double arch across the dark heavens. A vivid pattern of light and colour lay on the sombre hills where they came to earth. Perhaps I was in the mood for moralising, but they suggested that mystic union of matter and spirit— one taking colour from the other—which I feel to be the keynote of our imminent Renaissance. . .

A few days later, I went to Kyle by 'bus to see the Perth Theatre Company perform *The Merchant of Venice*. The journey was an entertainment in itself—the little vehicle packed with happy, laughing Highlanders (for the theatre in Kyle is something of an event!) The play was excellent; the hall filled to capacity. Indeed, though I am an ardent " Shakespeare fan," I have never seen a performance which succeeded better in holding the attention of the audience. As we came out of the theatre, I overheard one man telling another that " you can't beat Shakespeare "—a sentiment which was met, surprisingly enough, with wholehearted agreement on all sides. We returned home packed like sardines, singing, refreshed, and as good-humoured as a school-treat! I thought of many an apathetic city audience, and wished that our greatest dramatist might look down from his heavenly stage and witness the delight of the Highlands in his work.

So back to Nostie and my packing—for the weather had settled again, and I was off on the morrow into the high hills.

I had planned to tramp up the whole length of Glen Elchaig, and spend a week at the " Iron Lodge," discovering the more remote hill-lochs of Kintail. Fortune was smiling, for not only did I get an answer in the affirmative regarding accommodation, but my good neighbour, Mr. Ingram, had business in that direction on the day in question, and drove me up in his car.

The name, " Iron Lodge," had long fascinated me on the map;

and the place itself proved to be no disappointment. Lying well beyond Loch na Leitreach, at the very end of the green glen, the white house, with its red iron outbuildings, had a delightfully homelike atmosphere which gave me the sense of being at once welcome.

I scrambled out of the car, collected Jeannie and the baggage, and tramped over a wooden bridge. The road ended here, only a rough track running on and over the hills to Pait. Behind the white house, a waterfall leapt down the green hillside, and a few silver birches tossed their leaves in the sunlight. The hum of the vanishing car died along the lonely green glen.

Mrs. Munro met me at the gate, seeming really delighted with the few red roses I had brought her from my wild garden. She was young, slim and fair-haired, and Jeannie and I felt at once at home. In the clean, spacious kitchen, we sat down and I had a cup of tea and home-made oatcakes. A large grey cat got up from a chair by the fire and fixed Jeannie with a mesmeric yellow eye. This, I was told, was Snookie. His grey-and-white mother, Bonkie, peeped once round the door and promptly vanished. If Jeannie had not been on the lead, she would have vanished too! Though she would never harm a cat, the sight of one running has always proved an irresistible temptation. I gave her a short lecture on the position of guests as compared to residents, and she went and sat in a corner, glowering at Snookie under her eyebrows. He went out with dignity; but presently came round and pulled faces at her through the window.

After lunch and a chat, I put on my boots and went out for the afternoon, the still-sulky Jeannie at my heels. All around, the high green hills seemed to shut out the world. Looking back along the glen, we saw Loch na Leitreach lying at the foot of fierce Càrnan Cruineachd, and the yellow road running away back towards Killilan.

I decided, on impulse, to try the long, circular tramp over to Loch Cruoshie and back by Coire nan Each. We set off without further delay, as the day was already well-advanced.

The sun blazed down (after weeks of rain) as we trudged up the stony track. The foxgloves were fading; the spent bog-cotton hung limply on thin stalks bent by the wind. But already the bell-heather was beginning to patch the hills with glowing colour. I found two varieties of this—the vivid magenta and the larger-belled pale pink variety, with grey-green leaves.

The air was loud with the joyous rush of waterfalls among the rolling green hills. We took the rough north track towards Beinn Dronnaig. To our right, Aonach Buidhe (The Yellow Hill) rose into a blue sky. Behind us, the Iron Lodge sank down and down into a green hollow, drowsing away the sunny afternoon. We crossed a landslide of scree, and followed the steadily-climbing path away into the wilderness. Blue and pink milkwort blended with the purple of the heather. The hills were covered with a mantle of emerald green, streaked with the grey-purple of occasional outcrops of rock. A few trees, rowan, hazel and birch, clung along the courses of the streams.

We found serpent-grass in the gulley by the track, and a few spotted orchis, though these are rarer in this part of Kintail. Presently, the path descended to cross the burn—then up again to a height of 1,500 feet, still very rough going. We reached the summit-cairn; and looked out on to a desolate landscape of bare hills, brown, green and grey, with the sharp peak of Beinn Dronnaig in the centre, surmounted by woolly cloud.

Here, there were no trees at all—only one sprawling, whitened stump lying by the stream, like a horned dragon carved in grey stone. We found the remains of an old wall running down the hillside to a ruined bothy near the track. The hills became more brown, slashed with rock and dead heather. We swung away from the burn across the open plain. Once, a solitary hind bounded out of the heather and disappeared over a nearby rise. We passed another cairn, which had such a grotesque, human appearance that Jeannie made a wide sweep, barking at it furiously. I put a little stone on the top—a feather in its hat, for luck.

The sun, which had temporarily hidden itself behind a cloud, came out again. Mist mantled Beinn Dronnaig, but to the west the sky was a pale sea-blue. We crossed another burn, and trudged on over the flat, damp plain. Soon we found Loch na Maoile Buidhe—The Loch of the Yellow Promontory—a bare, heart-shaped pool reflecting nothing but the blue of the sky. It had no distinctive feature save a half-moon of bright green reeds in the centre of the still waters. It lies at a height of around 1,000 feet, in the midst of bleak, boggy ground.

The track now became very wet. Many of the wayside pools were covered with bright green weed. Over others, the water-beetles skated merrily, drawing zig-zag patterns on the peat-brown water. A striped frog swam strongly under overhanging " cliffs " of grey moss, its colours, with their hint of bloodless transparency, brought to life in the clear brown pool.

At length—a glimpse of bow-shaped Loch Cruoshie in the green flat-land ahead. Down in a calm valley, the River Ling wound out from the hills of Attadale Forest, flowing into the loch, and straggling on again into the wild green landscape beyond.

The Ling is the northern boundary of Kintail; and here we were on the fringe of our chosen " territory," looking down on the loch which lies half in Lochalsh. There are no trees around Loch Cruoshie, but, none the less, set in the shadow of Beinn Dronnaig, it has a certain wild beauty. It has several tiny islands and a hint of golden sand; and we found some old cottages and ruins along the shore.

The wind freshened as we took our tea, and puffy, sunlit clouds rolled in soft billows across the sky. We had a long drink from a brown stream—and then up again, to tackle the second, and more difficult, stage of our journey.

Swiftly, we tramped back to Loch na Maoile Buidhe. The sundew was feeding by the wayside, red and sticky among black peat. We left the path and splashed through marshland to the loch, then followed the stream winding away to the east. Soon, I was sinking ankle-deep into wet peat. To our right, water flowed down from the corries of Aonach Buidhe in a series of small linns. We climbed a rocky hummock and looked back over the marshy plateau, jewelled with a hundred tiny pools and streams, all shining like polished jet. In the moss at our feet, a species of bright red fungus gleamed like scattered rubies. Over the hills, a stray herd of deer galloped in leisurely fashion at the heels of a proud stag.

We climbed on—and presently we looked down on to the lovely string of lochs beyond Cruoshie—Lochan Góbhlach, Loch an Tachdaich and An Gead Loch. The first—The Forked Lochan—is in reality two distinct lochs of similar shape. Although this series of hill-lochs lie just beyond the boundaries of Kintail, I would not have missed seeing them for the world. They nestle in a deep, quiet valley—a long, lovely chain of shining waters, dotted here and there with tree-clad islands. Their height from sea-level is about 800 feet. Running away from them to the south is the vivid green cleft of Coire nan Each, where General Monk lost a coach and some horses in the bog on his way through from Perth to the West. The General had been sent by Cromwell in 1654 to overawe the Royalist clans, and reports having abandoned one hundred baggage-horses on his way through this treacherous pass. I have since been told an amusing story about some chocolate which was found in one of his captured coaches. Apparently, the Highlanders had never encountered such a preparation before, for it was finally listed in their inventory of spoils as " salve for rubbing on wounds "!

Considering the nature of his visit, General Monk seems to have shown admirable restraint while in Kintail, for there was only one man killed. This was our old friend Duncan MacRae who intercepted Angus Òg Macdonald in a galley at Kylerhea, and brought his body back to Eilean Donan Castle. Duncan was then an old man, and, a little while previous to General Monk's arrival, it had been prophesied that he should die as he had lived—by the sword. Duncan, however, refused to believe this, and consulted the famous Brahan Seer, who confirmed the prophecy.

Duncan was then living in Glen Shiel; and one day, while out on the hills, he encountered some of Monk's men, who spoke to him in English. Although he was very old, this so enraged him that he at once drew his sword, but was quickly overpowered by the soldiers and killed. So ended the life of the intrepid old warrior whose exploits were ever a source of pride to his clan.

Among the plunder taken by General Monk in Kintail was a large herd of cattle belonging to Mr. Farquhar MacRae, brilliant minister and Constable of Eilean Donan Castle. Relatively little damage was done at first, however, as the General had " other fish to fry," his real quarry being General Middleton, who had been instrumental in fostering the Stuart rising of 1653, under the Earl of Glencairn. The wary Middleton, however, had already left the district and gone to Glenelg. Thereupon, General Monk abandoned the pursuit and his men contented themselves with burning houses and stealing cattle " to make amends for the hard march "; after which the army departed towards Glen Strath Farrar. Shortly after this, the rising fell through. After the Restoration in 1660, Kintail was quiet until the time of Sherriffmuir.

The track through Coire nan Each, along which the horses came to grief, is part of the old Coffin Road from Pait to the burial-ground at Clachan Duich. The corrie itself is green and smooth, haunted by herds of shy deer. From a distance, the ground appears to be covered with rich pasture. It is only when you walk on it that you discover the treachery. The slopes overlooking this green valley are the first place in Kintail where I found the club-moss growing in anything approaching profusion. Even here, it grows patchily; but the roots are strong and the plant tall and of a bright yellowish hue.

We began our descent of the green flank of An Creachal Beag, looking across Coire nan Each towards a landscape of blue-shadowed, sun-washed hills stretching away into an infinity of gold clouds. To the north-east, the great grey ridge of An Riabhachan rose fierce against a grey-blue sky. The string of lochs vanished behind the curve of the hill, and we plunged down over the swampy ground towards the track far below.

Reaching the floor of the valley, I crossed the sandy river simply by wading across in my already-soaked boots. Judging from her expression, Jeannie thought I had sun-stroke—but, after a few re-assuring words on my part, she deigned to follow, with her long coat floating out on the tide and her short legs moving with the action of a swimmer in case she should be caught unawares in deep water.

Safely over, we trudged and splashed along the incredibly boggy path for perhaps four miles. Although it was now evening, there was still brilliant sunlight. At last, we crossed a small burn, and came to stones instead of swamp. By this time, we had had more than enough of Coire nan Each, and my sympathies were all with General Monk! Even the shy brown deer, fleeing gracefully up the hillside at our approach, had not compensated for the layers of mud through which we had floundered in an effort to follow the path.

Once on the stones, we made rapid progress to the summit-cairn. A few moments later, we reached Loch Mhoicean, 1,500 feet up, bare and still, reflecting only the green of the close-gathered hills, Càrn na Bruaich Bige, Aonach Buidhe and An Socach (The Snout). At the far end of the loch, we passed a shepherd's hut of grey wood, the sole reminder of civilisation on this lonely shore. Though bare and desolate, Loch Mhoicean looks interesting from a fishing point of view, and is a fair size, as hill-lochs go. It is quite easy to reach from Loch na Leitreach, as a road goes to the Iron Lodge and a goodish track covers the remainder of the distance. The route via Coire nan Each, as I have already remarked, is another story!

Passing the loch, we surmounted a rise—and there, in the distance, lay the blue expanse of Loch na Leitreach, with the black peak of Càrnan Cruineachd beyond, like a sentinel keeping watch over the deep green glen. Our path was now running close to the Allt na Doire Gairbhe, which flowed through a miniature gorge flanked with alder trees and ferns. Soon, we gazed down on to the Iron Lodge, shining white in the mellow light of the evening. The sight sent a thrill through me, for, already, I was thinking of the place as home. . . So quickly does the habitual wanderer adjust himself to new surroundings.

Jeannie began to wag her tail as we ran down the hill. She, too, seemed to realise that we would be sure of a welcome—or was it the thought of Bonkie that brought the eager light to her eyes. . ?

For myself, it was the sight of smoke drifting up in a blue plume on the still air which made me forget the ache in my feet. Anew, it seemed to me that the best part of going for a long tramp is the feeling that assails one at the end. I had been seven hours " on the hill," with one stop for a sandwich, and a great many irritating little pauses to make notes on my surroundings. I suddenly realised that I was hungry, thirsty, dirty, and ready for nothing so much as a long rest by a friendly fire.

In record time, I was down in the glen, across the bridge, over the threshold of the clean white house by the rushing fall. I was greeted by a welcoming smile from my hostess, a firm hand-shake from her husband, and a rapturous welcome from a collie puppy called Morag, who excited Jeannie's immediate jealousy, and diverted her attention from the cats. Having assured her that I still loved her best, and in some measure restored the peace, I took off my soaked boots and " relaxed " by the fire.

Supper followed—stew, oatcakes, scones and crowdie, with as much tea as I could drink. Jeannie was finally persuaded to take a dish of brose and some scraps of meat, the presence of Morag causing her to forget her dislike of eating in strange houses. While she took her meal, Bonkie and Snookie peered in at her through the window, their eyes as wide as saucers, while the " grown-up " collies, Fred, Jack and Sheila, peeped warily round the scullery door. Jeannie contented herself with curling a disdainful lip at the whole company—but I have never seen her make such short work of a large meal! Afterwards, she lay on the hearthrug, tense with suppressed wrath, while a curious Snookie circled round her trying to find out which end was the head and which the tail. The fact that her eyes were completely hidden by grey hair did not make his problem any easier—but the answer came with startling suddenness when Jeannie made a quick dive, sending him clawing and spitting on to a chair. Having thus, in her own mind, established the supremacy of dog over cat, she then went to sleep as calmly and easily as if in her own home!

Talk drifted on, quietly and happily, until the fire burned down to a dull red glow. On the rack above the highly-polished range, my boots lay drying for the morrow. Already, I was weaving plans, mapping out routes, drawing up a programme for each day. Above all, I was praying for fine weather! In this direction, particularly, Kintail is a land of surprises!

GRACEFUL LARCHES, INVERINATE

CHAPTER XI

LOCH LUNGARD AND THE HIGH HILLS

IT was as well that I had prepared myself mentally for the unexpected. The following day presented us with West Highland weather at its worst—a steady torrent of rain calculated to damp the spirits to match the state of the body.

For most of the day, Jeannie and I sat by the window, waiting for it to " clear." Outside, the yellow, swollen burns roared and leapt down the sodden braes, and the clouds spilled like a white foam over the grey hills. No ray of sunlight penetrated the mist to lift the pall of despair from the heart of the earth.

Mrs. Munro and I read, wrote letters, and did " odd jobs " about the house. Towards evening, before the cows came up for milking, we went out for a short walk.

The clouds by this time were rolling down about the feet of the hills. The wind had dropped, and there was no longer any rain—just a heavy, sultry stillness with the mist clinging in moveless veils over all the desolate land. We picked a few heads of the fragrant orchis and inhaled the scent, which resembled nothing so much as a field of blooming clover. Then Mrs. Munro found some bog-myrtle, and we rubbed it between our fingers, sniffing delightedly at the pungent perfume with its suggestion of eucalyptus.

All around us, the hills were hiding behind their still veils of vapour. Càrnan Cruineachd and Meall Scouman had vanished altogether. Loch na Leitreach (or Loch Carnach, as it is called locally), had turned from silver to a dull, leaden grey. Over all things, the loneliness of the waste land brooded like a spell. Only the wild burns, careering perilously over white stones, suggested the continuance of the pattern of life. Only here did the voice of the hills cry aloud, savage and full of old sorrows, singing its endless song of grief unassuaged.

We went in . . . And, presently, the clouds flowed thickly round the lonely white house, and Night came softly, clad in a grey cloak, over the hidden byways of the moors.

On closer acquaintance, Jeannie decided that the grey cat, Snookie, was " no' that bad, after all." On the morning of our third day at the Iron Lodge, she bounced rapturously up to him and licked his face. This brazen advance was promptly rewarded by a sound buffet on the ear—but, presently, the two of them were lying side-by-side on the couch, completely at ease and dead to the world!

I fear, though, that Jeannie has a rather Victorian attitude to children. It was soon obvious that, to her way of thinking, the baby collie, Morag, was sorely in need of discipline. Of the adult collie bitch, Sheila, she tactfully took no notice at all; but it was easy to tell that their attitude towards each other was that of two women sharing the same kitchen!

She still showed an alarming tendency to chase the timid Bonkie, and I was glad when a slight change in the weather afforded the opportunity of walking off some of her surplus energy.

We set out bright and early, emerging from the cosy house into a world glimmering with raindrops. The eyes of the sky were still heavy with unshed tears; but I was chafing to find those elusive hill-lochs and had decided to risk the possibility of a drenching.

We climbed up the flooded path behind the Iron Lodge into the sombre eastern hills. Heavy cloud began to roll in solid banks overhead. A cold wind whistled through the sparse bracken. Soon, a uniform greyness lay over the whole landscape, lighted only by the occasional purple flame of the bell-heather. Vast waves of mist boiled and swirled over the high hills.

Following the old right-of-way from Kintail to Glen Cannich, we came presently to Loch an Droma, a tiny ribbon of water at a height of about 1,000 feet. Little grassy hummocks and tufts peeped out of the drab green water, and behind the loch the drab grey cliffs of Sgùrr na h-Eige (The Notched Peak) ran up into the clouds. Loch an Droma means the Loch of the Ridge. It has a twin sister, which was not shown on my map. Away beyond the two of them, we could see the great north-east ridge of Sgùrr nan Ceathreamhnan (the Peak of the Quarters), and the dark hills around Loch Lungard.

Beyond the foothills of Sgùrr na h-Eige and Creag Ghlas, the forked burn rolled down from the cloud-hidden peaks, swollen with heavy rains, surging on its way to the misty expanse of Lungard. Away to the south, desolate Gleann Sìthidh ran up and round into mist and rain. We could see the track on the far side of the Amhainn Sìthidh, and the beginnings of Gleann a' Choilich, which I had hoped we might explore. Crossing the river, however, proved to be an impossibility without swimming, so I decided to tramp up An Fraoich Choire (The Heather-Corrie) to the lochan of the same name.

Heavy veils of rain were again sweeping over the hills as we set off across the peat-bog. Following the west fork of the burn, we came up into an arena of dark mountains half-swathed in cloud. My feet by this time were squelching in my boots, and Jeannie resembled nothing so much as a drowned rat. The climb seemed interminable. During the last stages, we scrambled up a steep gorge in the flank of Sgùrr nan Ceathreamhnan, straight into the clouds. Of what lay above us we had not the faintest conception. I would never have dared to attempt it had I not had the burn to guide me.

At 2,500 feet, we came so suddenly upon the loch that we almost walked into it. Cloud poured round and over us in great, wet billows, obscuring everything. According to our map, this loch was the highest we had yet visited, an oval pool lying in a semi-circle of high hills—but of these last we could see nothing. A few yards ahead of us, cloud lay heavy on the grey waters, blotting out the entire landscape. Despite the name of the corrie, we did not find a single root of heather. Underfoot was swamp, moss and sodden peat. There was no dry place to sit to eat a meal, and a cold wind chilled us to the bone. We blundered back to the burn and descended again to the foot of the gorge, where I ate a quick and belated lunch in pouring rain. Jeannie sat and shivered, refusing to share the damp sandwiches and looking in horror at the flask of brandy.

As quickly as possible, we slithered down into the valley and began to follow the stream back again, this time on the opposite side.

This manoeuvre, we discovered later, was a mistake. Towards the mouth of the corrie, the burn became so wide and strong that we could find no place to cross. Finally, I picked Jeannie up and waded it in my boots, fighting against the fierce knee-high current which was doing its best to sweep me off my feet. The slippery, uneven rocks underfoot added to the difficulty—but, at last, we were over, back on the path, and heading for home.

After a good night's sleep, we tried it again, having seen nothing of the loch the day before. This time, we crossed the pass just beyond Loch an Droma and climbed the crags of Sgùrr na h-Eige. We had been late starting, and it was afternoon when we reached the top. From here, we looked out on to the whole glorious panorama of north-eastern Kintail, with glens, streams, mountains and waterfalls on every side. We could see beyond Loch Lungard to where the river widens into Loch Frith an Acha and Lochan na Cloiche, with a hint of blue Loch Mullardoch behind, set among blue-black hills. North-west, we looked up into the cleft between Faochag and Aonach Buidhe, our now-familiar route to Loch Cruoshie and Coire nan Each. Away beyond this, the flat table-top of Bidein a' Choire Sheasgaich (The Pinnacle of the Reedy Hollow), lay under thick cloud. South-east lay An Fraoich Choire (our route of yesterday), Gleann Sìthidh and the now-clear ridge of Sgùrr nan Ceathreamhnan. The air was vibrant with rushing waters, and a sharp wind cooled us after the climb. Sunlight patched the tattered garments of the tired old hills.

We scrambled on to the ridge to the west, and looked away to Sgùman Cóinntich and the hills above the River Ling. Farther still, the Gleann Udalain summits loomed grey-gold against a watery sky.

We had a breath-taking view of Glen Elchaig—the grim black crags of Càrnan Cruineachd, the unnamed hill-lochs on the far side of Loch na Leitreach, and the kidney-shaped pool known locally as Loch a' Mhurachaidh (Murdoch's Loch) above Carnach and the Falls of Glòmach.

We found Loch Sgùrr na h-Eige at 2,250 feet, lying in a hollow at the foot of Creag Ghlas. A fierce wind whipped round us and lifted the tufts on Jeannie's ears. We found shelter behind some rocks, where we had tea. Dark cloud was now bearing down on us from the west. In a few moments, all the higher peaks were obscured.

" Jeannie, my lass," I said, regretfully, " we've had it ! "

But the cloud cleared in a few minutes, and the temptation was too much. It was " now or never " for the hill-lochs on this side of mighty Sgùrr nan Ceathreamhnan. I put away the remainder of the sandwiches, and we were soon ploughing along the scree-slopes of Creag Ghlas, the Grey Rock. A hen grouse shot suddenly up in our path and flapped away, feigning a broken wing. Jeannie, completely taken in, dashed in hot pursuit. I looked for the nest, but in vain.

We came round behind the summit of the hill, and looked down onto Loch Thuill Easaich, Loch Gaorsaic and the beginnings of Loch a' Bhealaich—the string of hill-lochs which I had already encountered on the Dorusduain route to Glòmach. Racing the cloud now, we climbed up on to the shoulder of Stùc Beag, on the west ridge of Sgùrr nan Ceathreamhan, whence I planned to descend at once if conditions became too bad.

The view from here was magnificent. Far below, gleaming silver through a faint pearly haze, the Amhainn Gaorsaic wound out from the hills and disappeared over the Falls. Below this again, the lovely green expanse of Glen Elchaig lay bathed in golden light, surrounded by a vista of golden hills bejewelled with tiny lost lochans uncharted on the map. On the far plateau to the west, Loch nan Eun glittered and danced under the caresses of a long bar of moving light.

We found the elusive Coire Lochan (2,500 feet) tucked cunningly away in a cloud-filled cleft—a little pool almost the shape of a star, with several tiny islets scattered across its quiet surface.

Cloud was now pouring towards us in a dense veil. Quickly, we crossed the gap between Stùc Mór and Stùc Beag and came out over An Fraoich Choire, where we huddled in a rocky crevasse out of the wind. Below, Loch an Fhraoich Choire blurred to a dull, misty grey. The landscape all around faded and was lost. We shared the rest of the sandwiches, waiting for the mist to clear. It was warm in our shelter, but we could see great eddies of wind sweeping over the loch below, drawing wrinkles and semi-circles on the leaden waters. But I was glad of one thing. To-day, it was possible to see the loch— a bare grey oval with only one tiny islet. It was also possible to check up on another point. There is no heather in the Heather Corrie! The only flowers I found were, of all things, a few sea-pinks and a white, starry creeper which also grows more commonly on the seashore.

The cloud had obviously come to stay, and further climbing was impossible. We therefore began our descent into the corrie, taking care this time to keep on the left-hand side of the burn. We arrived at the Iron Lodge at dusk, tired but happy, after seven hours on the hill.

And the next day was fine! And so, I thought, for the farthest of the hill-lochs of Sgùrr nan Ceathreamhnan—wee Loch Coire nan Dearcag, the Loch of the Corrie of Small Berries, set at 2,500 feet at the head of Gleann a' Choilich.

My long-suffering boots were dry again, and my good-hearted hostess saw to it that I had a large breakfast and plenty of sandwiches.

The last two days had tired me a little, though, and I was late starting. Jeannie was a little weary, too, but refused point-blank to be left behind. We were delayed again crossing the Amhainn Sìthidh, which was still high. It was 3.30 in the afternoon when we reached Loch Lungard with its lonely shepherds' bothy and brown-and-white cattle grazing along the shore.

We crossed the Amhainn a' Choilich by a flimsy bridge which quivered beneath our weight. Before us, desolate Gleann a' Choilich curved away into hazy hills; the north-east ridge of Sgùrr nan Ceathreamhnan on one side; Beinn Fhionnlaidh, Màm Sodhail and Càrn Eige on the other. We were now on the track which runs over from Lungard to Glen Affric; but we soon left the path to follow the course of the burn. Cattle were grazing peacefully along the banks of the stream—red and golden and white, with tiny, soft-eyed calves.

The glen seemed to go on for ever. We left the cattle far behind, crossed the burn again, and floundered into peat-bog and water-logged turf. The landscape became wilder as we progressed into the hills. Deer fled before us, or peered curiously over the skyline, as if astonished at our intrusion into this bleak, wild place. The glen, silent and lonely, curved round and up into a wilderness of crags, boulders and drifting cloud. Behind us, cloud dropped like a dark curtain over the blurring hills of Lungard.

The head of Gleann a' Choilich, when you finally reach it, presents scenery of appalling wildness and desolation. Riven grey rock—black peat—fierce crags, and great, dark peaks forming a semi-circle all around. The air was loud with the rush of angry waters. We saw many deer, which bounded silently away into the clouds at our approach. It was now 7 p.m., and I was tired and hungry, but still quite a distance from the lochan. I stopped for fifteen minutes for a meal. Then, a little refreshed and rested, we continued with our slow climb out of the head of the glen. At length—a gleam of vivid green—and there was the tiny lochan, covered with young weed, hiding in a hollow among steep grey cliffs and loose scree. Before us, the highest of the four summits of Sgùrr nan Ceathreamhnan, 3,771 feet, rose clear against a patch of blue sky. But we were again racing the cloud, which was pouring like a torrent over from Glen Affric, billowing and belching silently to our undoing. It was an exciting contest. There was no time to take notes, much less a photograph. The ground was full of tussocks, boulders and pot-holes, and a fierce cross-wind threw us off our balance, slowing us up considerably. We headed for the still-clear north-east ridge, tired and breathless, and it seemed that we would never make it! At last, we were past the 3,000 ft. level—up, over—and there, far below, lay Gleann Sìthidh, spelling peace and safety, stretching away dimly into blue and gold haze.

We plunged down, without pause, to the welcome gleam of the Amhainn Sìthidh. Behind us, the grey crags of the ridge rose higher and higher against the sky. Whatever happened now, we were safe at last from the treacherous cloud.

The circular tramp from the Iron Lodge via Gleann a' Choilich, over the ridge of Sgùrr nan Ceathreamhnan, and back by Gleann Sìthidh, is like following the curve of an enormous horse-shoe. The two glens are quite different—the first wide and sprawling, overlooked by grey crags and scree; the second steep, secret, shut in by close green braes evenly striped with blue furrows made when the hills were young. The only living creature we encountered in Gleann Sìthidh was a buzzard! Perhaps it is too lonely—or boggy—to attract visitors? Yet, this glen has a strange and haunting beauty; and the name of the burn—the Amhainn Sìthidh—seems to hold a suggestion of sleep and fine dreaming. There is a tiny lochan—An Lochan Gorm—near the source of this stream, which, set at just over 3,000 feet, rivals Loch a' Choire Dhomhain on Càrn Eige for the title of highest hill-loch in Kintail.

The climber who wishes to attempt this circular walk, however, should be prepared for three things—the possibility of high water in

the burns, mist on the ridge, and the effect of mile upon mile of wet peat-bog on one's energy and speed. I left the Iron Lodge at 1 p.m., and stopped for only fifteen minutes during the whole tramp. Nevertheless, I did not reach " home " again until a quarter to eleven—and that in a state of near-exhaustion. Mrs. Munro confessed herself on the verge of organising a search-party of one, but forgave me when she saw the state of my feet!

I dropped into a chair and consumed a phenomenal supper. Jeannie was too tired even to chase Bonkie! Outside, the blue shadows gathered and fell across the quiet glen, and the soft murmur of the waterfall crept like a lullaby across the hush of night.

Mr. Munro came in from the sheep, and the three collies peered curiously round the door, their eyes yellow in the circle of lamplight. Jeannie, stretched flat on the hearthrug, did not so much as twitch an ear.

I put my soaked boots on the rack above the fire. Poor boots— they had carried me well. And there was worse to come! My mind recoiled from the future and found solace in the present—in the somnolence of firelight and lamplight—the quiet, homelike atmosphere of this sanctuary in the Back of Beyond. With a sensation of peace and contentment which will be familiar to all who climb the hills, I stretched out my pleasantly-aching limbs to the warm glow of the fire.

And so to bed—with a memory of happy conversation, and a feeling of strength and quietude gathered from the silent places of the earth. Dreamily, my mind running over the adventures of the day, I lay for a long time listening to the murmur of the stream below my window. Jeannie snored shamelessly from somewhere near my feet. The darkness was close and friendly; but, though weary in body, I was mentally aware of every slight vibration of air from the open window, every

THE FIVE SISTERS OF KINTAIL. ON EXTREME LEFT CLACHAN DUICH, RUIN OF KINTAIL CHURCH WITH GRAVEYARD delicate change and inflection in the voice of the night. A flutter on the window—was it a moth's wing, beating vainly on the glass? A low, crooning note from the byre—the cow speaking softly to her young calf. A crackle of twigs where something moved stealthily in the stillness. Over all, the quiet hushing-song of the sleepless waters, a threnody of life and death, pain and passion, echoing all the sorrows of the world.

Slowly, my thoughts fell into the pattern—were crystallised into its sweet-sad rhythm:

> Blows the wind to-day, and the sun and the rain are flying,
> Blows the wind on the moors to-day and now,
> Where about the graves of the martyrs the whaups are crying,
> My heart remembers how! . .*

It was the voice of the beloved master, who said it all so much better than the rest of us. I lay still, the feelers of my still-wakeful mind reaching out into the dark—and, softly, the answer came back on the night wind:

> I hear the signal, Lord—I understand.
> The night at Thy command
> Comes. I will eat and sleep and will not question more.*

* From the *Poems* of Robert Louis Stevenson.

CHAPTER XII

BENULA AND BACK: THE LONGEST TREK OF ALL

IN his delightful book, *Gateway to Skye*, Mr. Duncan Macpherson recounts how, before the construction of Dornie Bridge, he had long supported a scheme originated by Mr. G. A. Mackay for the building of a road from Benula Lodge to Carnach. The great advantage of this would have been that one could then have reached Kyle of Lochalsh via Killilan, without having to cross Loch Long. The road, running along the line of the old right-of-way from Glen Cannich, would have provided a through route from east to west, and the idea seems in every way admirable.

But there is one point on which I must raise the niggling voice of the sceptic. The memorandum dealing with this project, as quoted by Mr. Macpherson, describes the distance from Benula to Carnach as being " only nine miles." Now, I am no authority on measuring mileage, but I have walked the distance, both ways, and (as some of my Chicago friends might put it) " it's a helluva long nine! "

Or was it measured in Skye miles which are said to be longer?

The sunlight twinkled over wet heather as I set out to find the far hill-lochs of Càrn Eige. I had left Jeannie behind, for I was afraid that this, the longest excursion of all, would be beyond her powers. (I was also afraid that it might be beyond mine, but that, as the saying goes, is another story!)

Mrs. Munro had packed me up a real trencherman's lunch, for I had no idea where my next meal was coming from, or under what conditions I should be spending the night. I had visions, all else failing, of breaking into the lonely bothy at Lungard, which would at least be preferable to the open hillside—particularly in view of the still unsettled state of the weather.

The Amhainn Sìthidh was still high, but I found a reasonably good crossing-place by a cluster of rowan trees. (After all, it was as well to keep one's feet dry as long as possible!) There is a good track on the south side of the stream, and I was soon down to the wooden bridge over the Amhainn a' Choilich.

From here, the track ran on, along the edge of Loch Lungard. According to the Rev. A. E. Robertson's discourse on the Old Tracks and Coffin Roads, the original route kept to the north side of Loch Lungard, where there are still a few ruined cottages. This, however, has now been abandoned, as the south route is far easier to follow.

As I approached the far end of the loch, the cloud began to lower over the hills, and a few drops of rain spattered on to the gravel by the shore. I put on my ancient raincoat, turned off the track, and began to climb up beside the burn flowing down from the heights of Càrn Eige. Behind me, the old cottage at Am Màm faded behind a wall of rain. A wing of wind swept and dipped across the loch, drawing silver streaks across the grey water.

Now I could see over the lower slopes to where the river widened into two swirling pools—Loch Frith an Acha and the slightly larger Lochan na Cloiche. Beyond this, it swirled over a shallow fall into Loch Mullardoch. Nestling against a dark triangle of pines, the gracious white lodge of Benula shone in fitful sunlight. Through my glasses, I could see signs of great activity—carpets lying on the lawn, painters wandering in and out of the French doors, and a tiny Cairn terrier which seemed to be in charge of the entire proceedings!

The sunlight spread across the green valley, shining on the white bridge over the river (a grand-looking affair from this angle); the road winding away along Glen Cannich; the bare grey ridge of Bràigh a' Choire Bhig, the first summit of Sgùrr na Làpaich, in whose secret corries lay the furthest of my hill-lochs. Following close upon the golden fingers of the sun, the dark shadows touched ben and brae, strath and stream, weaving their sombre patterns over all the quiet land.

An errant wind was drawing thin lines of foam along Loch Lungard, like furrows from a faery plough. I sat on a boulder and ate my sandwiches, revelling in the lovely scene.

Then I climbed on, up the smooth shoulder of Càrn Eige—up and up to the peat-filled corrie below the peak of Beinn Fhionnlaidh. Here, I was startled to see what I took to be patches of snow on the dark summits—but my glasses revealed them as outcrops of quartz and mica, making vivid splashes of silver-white on the grey-brown shoulders of the hills.

The lochan I was seeking lies on the top of a shelf of grass-grown rock. I climbed above it to the left, and looked down to where it nestled darkly in the hollow. It was bare and desolate, black with the reflections of the hills, devoid of sunlight.

After waiting, in vain, for the right conditions for a photograph, I crossed the ridge to the east in a sharp, cool wind. Now I looked along the whole sun-chequered length of Glen Cannich, with its string of lochs stretching away into cloud-filled distance. I had left the grass and heather behind, and was tramping over scree, through which blaeberry-shoots raised their young, orange-tipped leaves to the moving light.

Across the valley, the scree-slopes of Bràigh a' Choire Bhig shone pure silver where the sunlight glinted on a million particles of mica. Behind this great bare shoulder of the earth, the dark and austere crest of Craig Dhubh brooded among the clouds.

I now came round to the fearsome crags overlooking the Allt a' Choire Dhomhain. The cruel precipices of Tom a' Chòinich turned my heart over. To my right, the burn wound up into a hanging corrie high on the bosom of Càrn Eige. Between me and that corrie was a steep descent—an even steeper climb on the far side of a scree-filled pass. And I had imagined that my climbing for to-day was over!

I started off down the scree, picking the flat stones where possible. A blue mountain hare bounded up from the rocks at my approach. I envied her her long, swift legs and sure feet, and half-suspected her of being a witch in disguise.

At first, I had thought of following the course of the burn; but the glen below was waterlogged and bright with wet moss. To my left, little unnamed pools shone in the tops of high banks of yellow-green turf.

But before me was scree—and scree only, guarding the approach to this little, secret lochan which has a fair claim to being the highest of all the hill-lochs of Kintail. The only one approaching it for altitude is the infinitesimal pool at the head of Glen Sìthidh—and, even then, I am not so sure.

I was now trying to hurry, for there was still the problem of finding shelter for the night. The " scree-field " changed to chips of quartz and marble, making a drift of silver down the grey shoulder of the hill. Someone had marked a path with boulders, but I soon left it to cut straight up on to the ridge.

Behind me, the dark expanse of Coire Lochan lay untouched by the sun. It was now teatime, and the wind was getting keener. On the opposite slope, the scree-drift ran in fantastic whorls and ripples, like sand patterns left by some vast ebbing tide. I threw myself into the climb with a zest I was far from feeling. The cloud was coming down again, and I was alone in a strange land . . .

At last, spent and breathless, I attained the summit of the ridge, and looked down the sheer crags of Càrn Eige on to Loch a' Choire Dhomhain—the Loch of the Deep Corrie. The name suited it well, for it lies among great pinnacles of scree and rock, surrounded by weirdly-shaped crags and boulders—some having a strangely-human appearance, like the inhabitants of a lost world.

Lying flat on the top of the precipice, I looked over, feeling faintly sick from the height, waiting for the sun to allow me a photograph.

Over a dip in the grey cliffs opposite, I could see a range of rose-and-blue hills—the hills beyond Glen Affric. Eastward, I looked away towards Loch Meall a' Mhadaidh, one of the hill-lochs above Glen Strath Farrar. Above Loch Mullardoch, the great crest of Tuill Creagach ran up into the gathering cloud.

I can find no words to describe the panorama of blue-patterned hills and glens stretching away into infinity on every side. Such things have to be seen to be believed!

I got my photograph and finished my crowdie sandwiches. Then, down, down, on the first stages of the long descent. Past the grey crags and precipices—over the shining quartz, where a flight of sea-gulls rose into the air at my coming, white wings against the white drifts of powdered stone.

Off the scree, and down again, through long heather and wet grass. I was tiring badly now, my muscles growing stiff after the long climb. I did not dare to think what would happen if I failed to get lodgings for the night!

Down towards the darkening valley, the silver curve of waters below. Down to the far gleam of Loch Mullardoch with its pine-clad islands and rocky hummocks along the shore.

At last, I stopped for a brief rest by a stream. Something white was moving along the winding road far below. With the aid of my glasses, I saw that it was a white horse, carrying its rider swiftly in the wake of a lorryload of logs. Civilisation! For once, I felt a glow of thankfulness at the thought.

Down. Down into the darkening valley, a strained muscle throbbing now with every step.

Finally, feeling slightly dazed, I reached the ruin of a recently burnt-out house. Then across the bridge (not nearly so impressive at close quarters), up the gravel road, and through the iron gates of Benula Lodge. Never had the sights, sounds and smells of civilisation been more welcome.

Feeling like a tramp, I stumbled round to the back door and rang a bell. Within, the sound of voices and laughter ceased. An attractive, dark-haired girl came to the door. Yes, I could come in; but I must excuse the muddle, as the place was being redecorated in preparation for " the family's " summer visit. Yes, they might be able to find me a chair or couch for the night. . .

They found me a bed. Mrs. Forbes, the English-born housekeeper; Janet, the cook; the dark-haired maid, Lily—all excelled themselves in kindness to the untidy and grubby stranger who had dropped into their midst, as it were, from the summits of Càrn Eige. Soon, I was sitting before the kitchen fire, drinking endless cups of tea, recounting my adventures, being fussed over by five Cairn terriers. I was asked to christen a tiny black-eyed puppy, and suggested " Pixie " because of its big ears. The others were called Peter, Sìthidh, Frauchie, and General Patch. I liked Peter best. He was old, and seemed to have a sense of discrimination (by which I mean that he did not automatically take me for a burglar!)

Everywhere was the pleasant smell of new paint. Young men from Glasgow, singing merrily, came in and out of the kitchen while I was having supper. I was told they were all living in the house until the work was finished. I enquired discreetly about the possibility of there being enough hot water for a bath, and was told certainly, if the painters hadn't had it. (Fortunately, they hadn't.)

After a goodnight cup of tea, I retired to the pleasant, airy room placed at my disposal. There were two hot-water bottles in the bed.

The blue mountain night closed in. Outside, the wide river sang dreamily among the great, scarred hills.

I switched off the light and let the warmth work on my sore muscles. For once, I was too tired to give a thought to the morrow!

The room was full of a cold grey light when I awakened. Footsteps echoed with a bleak, hollow sound among the empty corridors downstairs. I dressed and went stiffly down to a breakfast of freshly-caught trout. My boots were dry. Everything was in readiness for the next part of the adventure—excepting me!

I cheered up a little over my second cup of tea. After all, the end of the excursion was in sight. What did a stiff leg matter? It would have been a good deal stiffer if I had had to spend a night on the hill!

Lecturing myself in this wise, I bade a reluctant goodbye to my kind benefactors, arranging to call back later for my pack. Then I went out into the cold wind, and plodded along the road towards the ridge of Bràigh a' Choire Bhig. It was then 10.30 a.m.

The sun began to come out. The wind dropped. Loch Mullardoch, with its tree-covered islands, had the appearance of a tropical lagoon under a blue sky. Outcrops of rock and mica began to gleam silver on the hills.

Before long, I realised that the climb was going to be hot work. It is impossible to predict the weather from one hour to another in these western hills.

I took off my heavy rain-coat and fixed it with a complicated system of straps over my shoulder. Just before Cozac Old Lodge, I cut off the road to the north and began to climb the ridge.

Imagine my feelings when, having spent the best part of two hours sweating up the first steep shoulder, I discovered that I could still see neither of the two lochs marked on my map! There was nothing for it but to go on to Sgùrr nan Clachan Geala (The Peak of the White Stones), the second summit of Sgùrr na Làpaich, a slope of loose scree which lived up to its name. Having come thus far, I would find those elusive hill-lochs or perish in the attempt!

I scrambled on, marvelling at my own folly. The hot sun now blazed down on to my back and shoulders. Great rocks which could have crushed me like an eggshell tipped and wriggled on the steep slope under my feet. There was moss on the scree, and I frequently put a foot right through it into a deep hole among the rocks.

I reached a cairn. There, just below, to the left, shone Loch a'

Choire Bhig, 2,500 feet up, with its two tiny islets and cloud-filmed ridge behind. But of the other loch I could see nothing. So now I must walk along the ridge. What a day! And I was still hoping to get back to the Iron Lodge by nightfall. . .

I started off again, pig-headedness taking precedence over wisdom. And, at last, following the long line of Coire Glas Liath, I found it, an oval expanse of shining water on the great shelf between high hills. This loch is only just inside the eastern boundary of Kintail, and is called Loch Thuill Bhearnach, or the Loch of the Notched Hollow. It is much more trouble to reach than one would imagine from the map—or perhaps my stiff leg made a difference to my outlook on this occasion.

I would climb Sgùrr na Làpaich again, though, if only for another glimpse of the view from the summit. Coming back, I stopped for a while by a cairn. Before me, away across Glen Cannich, Coire Dhomhain was filled with cloud. I could not see the little lochan I had visited yesterday, so cunningly was it tucked away in the folds of the hill.

But I could see Loch Beinn a' Mheadhoin in Glen Affric; and, in the far distance beyond Glen Strath Farrar, the great expanse of Loch Ness, like the sea, shining palest silver between dim green hills. Further still, a hint of pearl on the horizon marked the unidentifiable summits of the Cairngorms.

The wind was rising again as I started my descent (for some reason the Clerk of the Weather was to-day in as contrary a frame of mind as myself). I photographed Loch a' Choire Bhig across the scree-slope, then plunged on down to Benula.

Back on the road, I lay flat in the dust beside a small clear burn and drank deeply of the sunlit waters. I reached the Lodge at 4.30 p.m., and was at once provided with an excellent tea. By five o'clock, I was once more " on the road."

Before me, four young people pushed bicycles along the stony track to Lungard. We passed and repassed each other, exchanging greetings and comments. Finally, they crossed the river beyond the loch and went into the deserted bothy where I had planned to take refuge in an emergency.

I felt cheerful now. I had decided neither to rest nor eat until I was across the Amhainn Sìthidh, two-thirds of the way " home."

Reaching my usual crossing-point, I waded across in my boots, not bothering about the stepping stones. Then I sat down and devoured the tomato-sandwiches nobly provided by the staff at Benula. By this time, I was, without exaggeration, too tired to think. I had a long drink from the stream, and followed it with what was left of the brandy in my flask. This was a bad manoeuvre. I was already stupid with weariness and a slight " touch of the sun." Before me, the familiar crags of Sgùrr na h-Eige began to assume fantastic shapes. I stumbled to my feet and floundered along the path, seeing hill-lochs in every cleft and corrie of the wavering hills!

The last mile seemed like ten. I leaned so heavily on my stick that I brought up a blister on the palm of my hand. Tripping over rocks and ploughing through burns, I at length reached the brow of the rise above Glen Elchaig. The gleam of the Iron Lodge, shining through the green trees below, was the loveliest thing I had ever seen!

I almost fell down the brae. Below, I could see Jeannie playing on a patch of grass at the end of the house. I whistled. She looked up, gave an incredulous bound of delight, and wriggled under the fence. A few moments later, she was in my arms, licking my face as if I had been gone for a year.

Mrs. Munro came out to feed the hens, and stopped in amazement at the sight of me stuck half-way through the fence (I was too stiff to bend!)

" Well," she said, " I wasn't expecting you the night, and your bed's gone! You'll have to sleep in the byre! "

I told her I was asleep already, and had been so for the last five miles.

So, amid much pleasantry, we entered the house, and I " flopped " luxuriously into an armchair before the fire. The kettle sang on the newly-blacked range. I kicked off my soaked boots and socks and stretched bare, dirty feet out to the blaze. I could not resist looking to see if the soles of them bore the imprints of the nails in my boots!

· · · · · · · ·

I was still seeing hill-lochs when I went to bed.

So now you know, Mr. Macpherson, why I queried that " nine miles "!

CHAPTER XIII

LOCH A' CHLÉIRICH AND THE FIVE SISTERS

A FEW days later, I was back at the cottage, laying plans for a trip to Loch a' Chléirich, the Priest's Loch—now the only high hill-loch in Kintail that I had not seen. I had hoped to cycle down to Morvich, climb A' Ghlas Bheinn, and return in the same day. But, of course, on the very morning I had arranged to start, I awoke to find it pouring with rain!

So, instead, I stayed at home and did the washing. Somehow, I had had enough of getting soaked to the skin for the time being!

It was still raining hard when I finished my task, so I decided to put up a clothes-line in the kitchen. For this, I needed a nail. Having scoured around very thoroughly downstairs, I went up to the attic to see if there were any stuck in the beams.

And here, for a while, I lost all count of time. Wandering about in the semi-darkness, among cans of sheep-dip, tar and marking-irons, I blundered into a pile of steel traps, presumably left by the last tenant. To pass the time, I picked one up and examined it at close quarters. It was what is called technically a " gin-trap "—something with which I had previously had no acquaintance, though I had been given to understand that they were " very efficient." I sat down and tested the spring. I could hardly force it apart, using my two hands. Odd stories and fragments of past conversations drifted into my mind.

I remembered how, during the recent War, an Englishman who had served his country in the R.A.F. was proudly telling me how he had once trapped a badger in the Essex woods.

"They're powerful animals," he said, "and I didn't think one trap would hold him. So I set two, close together, in the hope that while he was dancing about with his foot in one of them, he might blunder into the other. And that was exactly what happened. . ."

"Do badgers do much damage?" I asked—to me, a logical enough question.

He shook his head. "Not in our locality. I just did it for the *sport*."

I murmured something inane in reply, feeling faintly sick. For a few days, his tale niggled unpleasantly at the back of my mind. Then I forgot it.

But I remembered it now. Once more, I tested the strength of the trap. It was certainly "efficient" enough, and could hardly fail to break the captive's leg—perhaps mangle it beyond recognition. And if no-one came by for a day or two. . .

Admitting that "vermin" are a "pest" and must be destroyed, I could not help wondering what they (or any other little dumb creature that supplies us with meat or furs) had done to deserve an end like this. Even the fox cannot help his nature.

And so, thinking of the enormous scale on which trapping by this (and worse) methods is done throughout the world, I sat there miserable and confused, holding the gin-trap in my hands. I am not a fanatic. I eat meat, wear leather shoes and sheepskin gloves. (But I will not wear a fur-coat, now, unless I know that the skins were obtained humanely.) I suppose I am an ordinary, slow-going Britisher who believes, however muddle-headedly, in the gradual evolution of order out of chaos, the triumph of Christian ideals in a civilised world.

Believing this, I began then to wonder if we could ever call ourselves civilised while we permitted barbarities like the gin-trap—if our dreams of a "New World" were not foredoomed to futility while the doors of our hearts remained closed against those of our fellow-creatures who could not speak for themselves. . .

Still pondering over the problem, I found my nail and went back downstairs. Outside, the rain had stopped at last, and a pair of rabbits were playing together on the wet grass by the little wall.

It is not given to us to take the law into our own hands. I just stood quietly in the doorway, looking at the little carefree things—and a ray of sunlight touched me and warmed me through and through, like the answer to a small private prayer. It came to me, suddenly, that perhaps my successor at the cottage, or my kindly landlord, would one day see those rabbits as I saw them—and perhaps he would be sufficiently moved by the sight to throw away the gin-traps and hunt with a gun, until the advent of humane trapping.

And now the last cloud had blown away, and I was able to put the washing outside. But it was too late in the day to think of climbing A' Ghlas Bheinn.

In the evening, I sent a message down to the Kintail Lodge Hotel by the driver of the Glen Shiel 'bus. Come what may, I must " do " my last hill-loch before the week-end!

The Kintail Lodge is a converted shooting-lodge, recently opened by the National Trust as a hotel. That is all I know about it, except that it is very comfortable and a splendid centre for climbers.

When Jeannie and I arrived on the evening 'bus, we were impressed at once by the easy, home-like atmosphere. Two children played gaily on the lawn, chasing a golden retriever puppy which mercifully managed to avoid the neat flower-beds. Beyond the little private road, Loch Duich gleamed orange in the sunlight, reflecting the black hulls of small fishing-dinghies heavy with piled-up nets in the stern. Behind the hotel, the wet rocks of Sgùrr na Mòraich shone like sheets of mica let into the flank of the hill.

We were shown to a comfortable room at the top of the house, and given sea trout and salad for dinner. Presently, we encountered Mr. Chisholm in the hall, and discussed the possibility of fine weather on the morrow.

Outside, the dying sun hung like a huge red lantern over the black-and-gold expanse of the loch. Cloud came lazily down over the dark hills of Glen Shiel, hiding the fierce crags of The Saddle, folding the chaste Sisters away behind a veil of blue mist. In the dusk, we walked along the pebbly beach, inhaling the pungent odour of wet seaweed—and, while Jeannie looked on in amazement, I indulged in the childish pursuit of shell-hunting until it was too dark to see.

Then I went back to my dainty green-and-primrose bedroom and set about oiling my boots.

The morning dawned misty, but fair. I had a large breakfast; then gave the boots another coat of dubbin. I had a strong suspicion that the hand of Fate was upon them, and they were not much longer for this wicked world.

We were away from the hotel by ten o'clock, tramping down the road towards Morvich in a quite unexpected shower of fine rain. Before us, the great, uneven ridge of Beinn Fhada blocked the eastern sky, looming ever closer like a dark fortress set between the clefts of Glen Lichd and the Bealach to Glen Grivie. The air was hot and sultry, the field-flowers drooping or dead save for vetch, cow-parsley, butter-cups and a few starry-eyed daisies. But, already, the ling was budding, though as yet it showed only the merest points of mauve among the brown and green foliage.

The River Croe was high with the recent rains. Along the green valley to the east, a white cluster of cottages marked Innis a' Chrò, the territory at the west end of Beinn Fhada, between the river from Dorusduain and that of Glen Lichd. Near the junction of these rivers, there was once an enclosure for cattle—a coop or " Crò "—hence the name of Crò Chin-t-sàile. Here, also, was the first church built in Kintail. Another suggested reason for the name Crò Chin-t-sàile, as explained by my friend, Dr. Farquhar MacRae of Ratagan, is the lie of the land around the head of Loch Duich, a flat valley surrounded by high hills, giving the impression of a coop or cattle-pen. The dominating mountain of this scene, Beinn Fhada (pronounced Ben Attow) is seven miles long. The name, "a' bheinn fhada," means "the long hill," and the mountain extends from the fork of the River Croe to Glen Affric.

But it was not on mighty Beinn Fhada that our thoughts were centred to-day. Half-behind him, and a little to the north, the scarred slopes of A' Ghlas Bheinn—The Grey Mountain—loomed dimly through the rain. It was in the shoulder of this steep hill, at a height of around 2,750 feet, that we expected to find the only high hill-loch of Kintail which remained unvisited. And, judging from appearances, we should have a stiff climb in very uncertain weather. It was far from encouraging to watch the top of our chosen mountain slowly fading into white cloud!

But, as yet, we could tramp on in comfort, without worrying about the future. On either side of the wet road, patches of bright, friendly jade mingled with the yellow-green of ripening hayfields. Sheep, newly-shorn, dotted the hillside above Ruarach with startling white. Drifts of pale grey mist swirled and vanished and reappeared again in the corries of the nearer hills, constantly on the move, as if to reassure us that they had not come to stay.

We followed the rough road from Ruarach towards Dorusduain. Gently, the hills began to close in, and the Grey Mountain loomed dimly through the rain, shadowed by the dark olive of its pine-plantations.

At the Dorusduain Lodge, we went through a gate bearing a Forestry Commission sign and a warning about fires. Then we branched immediately away to the right and crossed a wooden bridge over the fast-flowing burn.

And now we were plunging through long wet grass, bracken and young pine, following a boggy track along the foot of the hill. The going was very wet, and I was soon soaked to the knees. The air remained hot and damp, with only the lightest breath of wind. Before long, I was sticky, breathless and irritable. Flies buzzed incessantly over the swamp, and midges contributed their unwelcome attentions to my perspiring face. The path crossed another burn, and plunged darkly downward among dripping trees. The forest seemed to be holding its pine-scented breath, waiting for something to happen.

The water off the trees splashed down my neck. Red and orange toadstools made little points of fetid heat in the heavy grass. We emerged from a dark patch of the plantation to see cloud hanging low over Beinn Fhada and rain slanting down on to bent grass and sodden earth.

Then we dived under more trees, and the ground underfoot became treacherous with boulders and long heather. At last, we reached a wire fence, the boundary of the plantation. It was a particularly strong and artfully-made fence, and we were some time finding a weak spot through which to scramble. After a long drink as a reward for our efforts, we struck steeply up the flank of A' Ghlas Bheinn, following the burn which, if my calculations were correct, would lead us straight to Loch a' Chléirich.

Heavens, but that hillside was steep—and wet! The burn frothed down through a fierce gorge, and we followed it as best we could. Behind us, mighty Beinn Fhada shut out the sky, and the white house of Dorusduain lay in a deep, dark hollow. To cheer us up a little, the sun came out, and spread a mist of gold over wet green and grey hills. Along the opposite hillside, the right-of-way to Glen Affric wound on towards a silver waterfall.

I felt better-tempered now, and rather hungry. The cloud seemed to be lifting from the hill-tops, though they were still dark with the shadow of it. A blessed wind ruffled the bracken and dried the sweat on my face. I called to Jeannie, and we climbed on with fresh heart.

I hope no-one will be " fooled " by the shortness of the distance to this loch as shown on the map. The steep climb more than makes up for it! Soon, Jeannie and I were doing it in brief spurts with short rests in between—and we were still exhausted long before we reached the top.

During one of these rests, I looked back at the magnificent tapestry spread out below. Beyond Dorusduain, the yellow road wound down to the head-waters of Loch Duich, surrounded by black-shadowed hills. Raising my eyes from this, I saw, on a nearby mountain-side a herd of the rumoured wild goats of Kintail, led by an enormous grey and black Billy with a flowing coat and great horns curving over on to his shoulders. The story of these goats is that they were once kept as domestic animals by an old woman of the mountains, but went wild after her death.

We climbed on, to the top of the ridge. From there, we looked away over the pass to the dim hills beyond Glen Affric. Rain was again blurring the surrounding landscape, so we turned northward and, at last, found our loch, a long, bare pool set between grey crags. After another rest, we climbed a rock-face to be in the right position for a photograph should the sun decide to emerge from its retirement once more. And, at length, after waiting an hour, I got a picture, the best it was possible to do under such uncertain weather-conditions.

On a fine day, Loch a' Chléirich would be a stiffish but enjoyable climb. Walking from the Kintail Lodge, it took me four hours to reach the ridge above the loch. This, however, is slow. A good climber should do it easily in three.

From the hill behind it, one can see north to Loch Carron, Skye and the Cuillin, and there is a fine view of the strange, flat-topped mountain on Raasay. Across Loch Duich lie Sgùrr Mhic Bharraich and Màm Rattachan, with the rough road cork-screwing up and over towards Glenelg.

We descended by the most direct way—straight down the steep face of the hill, avoiding the crags on the right-hand side of the burn. Clouds of pale moths fluttered up from the bracken as we gained the lower slopes. In just under an hour, we were back at the forest fence, and I was drinking out of my mackintosh hat beside the swift stream. Gone now was my irritability of the morning. Renewed contact with the hills had refreshed and strengthened me—as always, given me a sense of re-discovering remembered beauty. I looked at Jeannie, and snapped my fingers—and she wagged the ever-ready tail. Peace in our hearts, we set off gaily along the forest trail towards the Kintail Lodge.

Of course, I could not leave the head of Loch Duich without trying a scramble on the Five Sisters. And for this, as luck would have it, we were blessed with a good day.

But we were too late starting to get more than a passing acquaintance with these lovely and famous hills. Along the side of the tree-fringed Shiel River, we wandered through a herd of young bulls which looked at us in such a manner as to side-track us for some time from the marked path. Presently, however, we were scrambling up the flank of Sgùrr nan Saighead, the Peak of the Arrows, looking across a green chasm to where the great, pure crest of Sgùrr Fhuaran rose into a clear blue sky. I had hoped, at first, to climb this hill—but was glad I didn't, as the view of it from this angle was something I felt the better for having seen.

Below us, the shallow, sandy river looped and wound through the green glen. A puff of wind stirred the waters of the irregular lochan, and moved the quiet reeds. About this loch, the Brahan Seer prophesied: " When Loch Shiel, in Kintail, shall become so narrow that a man can leap across it, the salmon shall desert the Loch and the River Shiel." Certainly, it is narrow now, in places, but hardly, I think, to the state described by Coinneach Odhar.

From Sgùrr nan Saighead, too, we could see the road over Màm

Rattachan, a yellow stripe flung willy-nilly across a purple hill. And, beyond, great waves of blue, cloud-shadowed crests ran away towards the islands, and down beside the deep gulley of Glen Shiel, merging with the dark ridges of the Saddle and the higher hills behind Sgùrr na Sgìne.

Massed white clouds sailed inland from the west. But still Sgùrr Fhuaran leaned against a clear, sunlit sky, and brilliant sunshine touched the black cliffs of Sgùrr na Càrnach behind. The bracken was browning, but blue scabious bloomed in the crevices of the rocks.

We ran into some bad scree, and worked slowly back and along the knobbly flank of Sgùrr na Mòraich. Far below us now, cars and buses ran along the Glen Shiel road, their enamel shining as it caught the sun. The noise of their engines filled the whole valley, echoing and re-echoing from the high hills all around. We were so high that they seemed to be crawling, like beetles engaged in a pitiful race from one point to another.

At the head of Loch Duich, the tide was now coming in fast, covering the sand-banks and patches of wet weed. We scrambled down over the tussocks and grey rocks, and, in the declining light of evening, once more reached the floor of the valley.

Having circumvented the bulls, we took the homeward path by the smooth river. A herd of Highland ponies stared at us from a fenced-in field across the stream. They were of every intermediate shade between white and black—and loveliest of all were the buffs, greys and creams with their dark points and flowing manes and tails. They were all slim, fleet and very glossy, with small heads and delicately-moulded legs. The thought occurred to me that it was probably a daintily-built animal such as these that had the task of carrying Dr. Johnson over Màm Rattachan. If so, no-one should have evinced any surprise at the difficulties of that ride!

In striking contrast to both Johnson's and Boswell's impressions of the journey through Glen Shiel are those of the Free Church minister,

Dr. Alexander Beith, who, in company with his colleague, Dr. Candlish, drove a pony-trap through this deep glen one dark night in 1846, on his way from Fort William to visit " Lillingston of Lochalsh." Dr. Beith's impressions of Glen Shiel by night are recorded poetically in his *Highland Tour* :

No stars appeared, and though they had, the horizon was too limited for our seeing many of them. Those who have travelled in the dark the road along which we were now advancing know how deep the darkness is made by the shadow of the stupendous mountains which enclose it, Scour Ouran, the mighty monarch of the vast wild, crowning them all. . .

It was long past midnight when we arrived at Shielhouse Inn, in the district of Kintail, and not far from the head of Loch Duich. . . Not a sound of any kind could we hear, unless it was, amidst the deep silence, the occasional feeble, responsive bleatings of sheep and lambs on the far-off hillsides. Not a dog even barked or moved his tongue . . . The house seemed to be under the power of enchantment, such as the *Arabian Nights* describe. . .

After repeated efforts to gain admission, the two travellers climbed in through the kitchen window. At 5 a.m., they were again on the road, heading over Màm Rattachan; and it was a beautiful Autumn morning . . .

The mountains, as we looked back, and as we looked to the north and south, were clear, sunlit, from their summits downwards; fleecy clouds rested on their deep bosoms; lights and shadows were never so strikingly contrasted. Loch Duich lay, far below, like a vast sheet of plate-glass, dark, motionless . . . All was stillness and apparent peace, Scour Ouran still the presiding monarch of the scene. . .

Each of the Five Sisters of Kintail, at close quarters, has a distinct personality of her own. Austere, proud and haughty as a legendary princess of the isles, Sgùrr Fhuaran towers above her companions, more often than not veiling her lovely head in the clouds. There are two stories concerning her name—one version having it that she was christened after Saint Oran, and the other that she is properly called " The Peak of the Well." There are a variety of spellings, and it is difficult to ascertain which story is the true one.

Her neighbour, dark Sgùrr na Càrnach, the Peak of the Rocks or Cairns, broods over the glen with the enigmatic, gnarled countenance of an old witch. Her rough, rounded crest is in striking contrast to Sgùrr Fhuaran's chaste purity of line.

Quite different again, is Sgùrr na Mòraich—a sprawling, spreading mass of lumpy rock, seeming to have no shape at all, or too much in the wrong places, like the Fat Lady at a circus. This hill is a particularly tiring one to climb. Its name means The Peak of the Sea-Marsh, and it was doubtless so called because of the view of Loch Duich head from its summit.

Sgùrr nan Saighead is just a long, scree-covered ridge, until seen from a distance, when it mysteriously takes on a conical outline to match its fellows.

Grimmest lady of the quintet is, as the name suggests, Sgùrr na Ciste Duibhe—the Peak of the Black Chest, or Coffin. The finest view of her sombre and evil beauty is to be had from the watershed in Glen Shiel, near which point she is first glimpsed by the traveller from Cluanie, scowling darkly through her clouds.

There is another hill in this range—Sgùrr nan Spainteach—but this one stands farther back than her companions, and climbers tell me that she is not usually numbered among the famous Sisters. As her name reveals, this lady had connections of an unforgettable nature with the Spanish troops in 1719. Perhaps that is the reason why, ignored by her sisters, she still keeps discreetly in the background?

There are other spellings of these names, but I have given here the ones most commonly used on maps, to avoid confusion for the stranger.

There is a story about Sgùrr Mhic Bharraich, on the opposite side of Glen Shiel, which is of interest to the student of Highland history. It was in a corrie near the top of this mountain that the Lochaber cattle-reivers used to hide their stolen herds the first night, in the conviction that no-one would think of searching for them at such a height. A corrie in the face of this hill is still called Coire na Laoigh, or the Calves' Corrie.

Climbers on the Kintail hills should be warned of one thing. They are rough, and, in places, covered with scree. Unless one is an experienced hill-walker, it is unwise to try to climb to the summits alone.

KINTAIL PEAKS IN GLEN SHIEL. REFLECTIONS

CHAPTER XIV

WEST COAST WANDERINGS

RETURNING to Nostie Cottage, I found a telegram waiting. My sister was having her first holiday for four years. Like many another war-weary seeker after peace, she was planning to spend it in the Highlands. She would arrive in Kyle of Lochalsh the day after to-morrow.

I tidied the cottage, rang up the grocer and the butcher, booked dinner at the hotel for the night in question, then set about studying maps. She had ten days, and it was her first visit to the West Coast.

Later, I went out to the telephone-kiosk again, and rang up ten hotels or boarding-houses in the Isle of Skye, drawing a blank at each!

Thursday came, and Jeannie and I met the train at Kyle. Of course, on that particular day, it was pouring with rain! And I had told her that the ride from Inverness to Kyle was " through some of the loveliest country in the world "!

She did not seem too depressed, though. Someone had lent her a map on the journey, and already she had a good idea of " the lie of the land."

We took the 'bus back to Nostie and discussed our plans over tea. Kintail first, with two days at Dornie. Then Mallaig, Armadale, Sligachan, back to Kyle, and on to Achnasheen, Kinlochewe, Loch Maree and Gairloch. An exhausting programme? Pooh! With a pretence at nonchalance, we snapped our fingers at it. My sister works for an American newsreel company—and I? Had I not recently tramped the whole of north-eastern Kintail in a week?

Of course, we carefully avoided any mention of where we were going to *sleep* during our West Coast Wanderings. After all, why bother about little things like that? I had been told repeatedly that there was "no accommodation whatsoever," so it was just a waste of breath to discuss the matter any further!

We collected Jeannie, suitcases, raincoats and maps, and went down to the hotel. For two nights, at least, we would have a shelter over our heads. For the rest, we would depend on the hill-fairies to take pity on two scatter-brained worshippers at the shrine of Beauty. Or, to put it in crude twentieth-century language, we would "jolly well trust to luck"!

The next day, it was still raining. The hills of Kintail glowered dourly at us through muddy grey cloud. Towards evening, we walked along the north shore of Loch Duich, gazing down at the grim grey waters, trying to pierce the veil of mist that shrouded the far vista of Skye and the isles. It was no good. Kintail was simply not playing the game. The Five Sisters had quarrelled and gone into a sulk; the trees wept in a wet wind; the magic mirror of the loch would reflect nothing but the brooding skies. We turned back, wind-blown and splashed with mud and rain, and found consolation in a satisfying dinner at the hotel and a lazy hour or two before the fire.

In the morning, we piled once more into the little 'bus and jolted into Kyle. The Five Sisters are as feminine in temperament as in name, and perhaps if we showed them that we just didn't care for their moods anyway. . .

Sure enough, when we reached the rise above Balmacara, and looked back, there they were, lifting their cloudy veils and flirting with the Sun-God, lovely as a summer dream of pale nymphs rising naked from a shadowy pool.

"Come back—come back. . ." they called; but the 'bus sped on over the brow of the hill, and only a breath of wind stirring among the waterlilies of Lochan Iain Òig carried their soft sigh of regret.

We came down to the blue sea, the scattered islands running out into a mist of gold. Mauve shadows lay heavy on the Cuillin. Sgùrr Alasdair was crowned with cloud. A few stray gulls dipped over dancing waves. The quiet houses of Kyle—some freshly-painted in black and white—looked out over sunlit street and shimmering water. People went leisurely in and out of the little shops. The London train was due to leave in half-an-hour, and reluctant " hikers " trooped, heavy-laden, towards the station.

A steamer-siren blared and shivered across the water as we went down to the quay. Jeannie was all for diving off the side of the pier. We succeeded in calming her, however, and were soon safely aboard.

Gold light scintillated diamond-wise on blue water. The passengers crowded on to the scrubbed decks. Young and old, neat and shabby, trippers, " locals " and weather-beaten wanderers with the loneliness of the sea in their eyes. Demobbed servicemen, a little self-conscious in their " civvy " suits. Women, over-dressed and under-dressed. Dogs and children, romping together on the clean boards. Walkers, cyclists and climbers, all easily identifiable by their shoes. Occasionally, a sailor or steward passed, with a queer rolling gait, and a pitying glance for the crowd.

The siren boomed again. The gangway rattled in. Slowly, the *Loch Nevis* drew away from the pier. A puff of salty wind swept across the decks, and the older people tucked tartan rugs around their knees.

A whirr of wings churned in the wake of the ship. Black-backed and black-headed gulls, grey gulls and herring-gulls, soared over the masts and round the bright red funnel. Some children threw scraps of cake into the water, and they vanished seaward in a flutter of grey and white, screaming over the coveted titbits. The little black-headed gulls soon fell behind; but the others rode powerfully on the wind, scanning the decks with fierce yellow eyes.

The ship throbbed through the narrows of Kylerhea, where a

launch brought passengers out from Glenelg. We looked across to the bay with its hotel and white houses, and the beginnings of the road over Màm Rattachan. Behind us, the ferry chugged over to Kylerhea on the ancient route to Skye, over which cattle and sheep used to be swum at slack tides until comparatively recent times.

Now the last of the passengers was aboard—the launch drew away —and we were off again down the open Sound.

Past the Sandaig Islands and the great, dark sweep of Loch Hourn. Past Ornsay, with the picturesque lighthouse on Eilean Sionnach. On our left, Beinn na Caillich and the green hills of Knoydart. To our right, the blue curve of Knock Bay, with the road running up over the brae.

A white-coated steward came along the deck, ringing a bell. We went down and had lunch. I sat next to a fair-haired young man in kilt and plaid of a rich blue and green tartan. I asked him his clan. He smiled, and said he was English, but had a great affection for the Highlands. Hopefully, I asked him why. He said " because of the pubs! " and went back to his haddock-soup.

This reply effectively silenced me for the rest of the meal.

At 12.45 we steamed into Mallaig. The whole place seemed to be covered with gulls. A small island offshore was a mass of seething white. The smell of kippers met us as we stepped ashore.

But the little town was lovely in the sunlight, its streets crowded with visitors. We wandered round, " window-shopping," until we found a place that served cups of tea. A train came in at the station, and more crowds flowed into the street, heading for the pier. We finished our tea and joined the throng. Brief though our visit had been, we had seen (and smelt) Mallaig, and the experience would be pleasant to remember.

A churn of waters, and the boat was away again, crowded this time to capacity. We did not need to be told that it was the time of the Glasgow Fair! A mass of happy, seething humanity packed the now-soiled decks of the *Loch Nevis*—hung over the rails—chattered and laughed and pointed delightedly to the blue hills of Rhum as we began to cross the Sound.

"Passengers for Armadale! Any more passengers for Armadale!" shouted the steward. "This way, please."

I milled through the throng to queue for tickets.

. . . And now came that strange feeling upon me of slipping back into olden times; and my ears were charmed again by the echo of the old sagas, the wavering, hollow sound of voices drifting across calm waters in time to the splash of oars.

And over all, a threnody of unassuageable grief, echoed the song of fair Bragela, mourning in the Isle of Mist for the great Cuthullin, who would come to her no more:

. . . It is the white wave of the rock, and not Cuthullin's sails. Often do the mists deceive me, for the ship of my love! when they rise round some ghost, and spread their grey skirts on the wind. Why dost thou delay thy coming, son of the generous Semo? Four times has autumn returned with its winds, and raised the seas of Togorma since thou hast been in the roar of battles, and Bragela distant far! Hills of the isle of mist! when will ye answer to his hounds? But ye are dark in your clouds. Sad Bragela calls in vain! Night comes rolling down. The face of ocean fails. The heath-cock's head is beneath his wing. The hind sleeps, with the hart of the desert. They shall rise with morning's light, and feed by the mossy stream. But my tears return with the sun. My sighs come on with the night. When wilt thou come in thine arms, O chief of Erin's wars . . ?

This is no place to renew the old controversy over the authenticity of James Macpherson's translation of the *Poems of Ossian*. In any case, I have not sufficient knowledge to advance an opinion. I can only say that, for me, the above quotation from *The Death of Cuthullin* sums up the whole dark enchantment of Eilean a' Cheò, and I cannot read it without a catch of the breath and a lift of the heart. . .

It seemed no time at all before we were ashore and in the 'bus, rattling up the leafy lane towards Teangue.

We got off at Knock, of which I had the happiest of memories.

With a prayer to the hill-fairies, I trudged down to the farm. As I had thought, they were full up. But, to cut a long story short, they " managed." It was arranged that we should have meals at the farm and sleep at the Manse.

After tea, we went down to the shore and scrambled over sunwashed rocks covered with lichen and sea-pinks. Above us, the ruin of Knock Castle loomed gloomily against the sky. The tide came in and chased us off the rocks. We climbed up to the castle and lay on a couch of soft turf, looking out over the sparkling sea, saying little, for there was little to say. . .

Next morning, leaving our cases at the Manse, we took the 'bus to Sligachan. It was a heavenly ride. The sea was blue again; but great, fluffy clouds hung over the high hills. The 'bus was crowded—indeed, when it stopped to pick us up, the conductor had asked us if we could " put it off until to-morrow "!

People looked curiously at Jeannie. Several asked what breed she was! Indeed, it seems that even in the dog world, a prophet is not without honour except in his own country!

The road wound in and out along the coast. Down Loch Ainort and up again. Past scattered grey crofts and under the shadow of scree-covered hills. Scalpay slid behind—Raasay, with its weird flat-topped mountain, loomed close across the dancing waters of the Sound.

Down Loch Sligachan now, at the feet of mighty Glamaig—and, at last, we rattled down to the Sligachan Inn—and it had just started to rain.

We saw the Cuillin, though, and walked for an hour along Glen Sligachan towards the great lift of Marsco and the high hills. Most fantastic of all was the notched peak of Sgùrr nan Gillean—a sight to stir the hearts of all whose feet ache for a climb. There was something sinister about the Cuillin to-day, though, for it was exactly a week since the young Englishman, Captain Marriott, had gone out alone and failed to return. Widespread search had been made for him the day before; but it is known among climbers that these hills do not readily give up their secrets. . .

We turned back, silent under their sombre spell. The 'bus came along the white road from Portree. It was raining quite heavily now, and the Cuillin loomed desolate and stark through a lowering pall of cloud.

We said little until we reached Broadford Bay, where cheerful white houses, blue sea, and the low, rolling moors ahead drove away the dark spell of the Black Hills. . .

And the next day, up bright and early, we took the 'bus to Kyleakin. It was a slow ride, for the vehicle stopped at scattered outposts to collect the mail. But it had its reward. At Isleornsay, we came upon a picturesque and enchanting scene—a young girl of breathtaking loveliness, sitting on the ground outside the hotel, between two curly-headed young fishermen of the same standard of good looks. The girl was tossing her long plaits, laughing and talking, while the men sat easily beside her, the sea-wind lifting their curly hair under the blue peaked caps. Beside them sat a minister, perched nonchalantly on an old box. In the foreground, the green grass, the rocks, the shining sea, the lighthouse bright in the soft light of early morning. Behind, the great, purple slopes of the hills.

It was a delightful scene—but something was wrong. What was it. . .?

" Why," said my sister, suddenly, " the girl's face is *thick* with make-up! "

" Why! " I gasped, in the same breath, " the minister is *chewing gum*! "

You are right. We had blundered into the cast of *The Brothers*, L. A. G. Strong's novel which was then being filmed on the Isle of Skye. Even as we watched, a large car drove up and out stepped a very capable-looking gentleman who, we presumed, was the director.

Along the lane came a flock of long-horned Highland sheep, driven by an old shepherd. Oh, that we, too, could have been conscripted as " extras," if only to have an insight into the mysterious world of the screen!

But the merciless 'bus drove on, away back to the road, away to Kyleakin, and we did not even see the " shooting " of one tiny scene.

And now began the second stage of our adventure, among country linked in history with affairs and traditions of Kintail. From Kyle of Lochalsh, we took the evening train to Achnasheen, and spent the night at the comfortable Station Hotel. Next day, after an early lunch, we piled into a large 'bus and sped northward and westward to the fair land of Flowerdale.

How stealthily the ling comes to life upon the hill! Throughout the golden Spring, the first, blue, hazy days of Summer, the great slopes of the Western Highlands remain sombrely brown, patched only by the old scars of riven rock.

Then, one morning, when the sunlight flows warmly into dark clefts and crevices, it seems as if the faintest mist of purple overlays the brown—but one can never be sure that it is not just a trick of the light.

Day follows day; gold follows gold. Slowly, almost imperceptibly, the mist deepens, the hills begin to blush as if under a remembered caress. . .

Then, with the red of the rowan-berry, the delicate chalices raise their bowed heads to the light—and it is a Summer afternoon, and the ling-heather is in bloom at last upon the high places of the earth.

Such an afternoon marked our arrival in the fastnesses of Glen Docherty. The road ran up over the brae—and there, blue in a blue hollow, lay Loch Maree, dotted with dark islands, fringed with feathery pines.

We sped down and down to Kinlochewe. White houses rose to meet us out of the valley. We stopped to take in more passengers at

the Kinlochewe Hotel—then on again, along the shore road, under arches of green, waving trees.

Soon, we looked across Loch Maree to the great crags of Slioch, over which hung banks of the whitest of white cloud. A waterfall poured in a thin thread of silver down a grey gulley, widening as it reached the loch. Across the water, we saw the village of Letterewe, hugging a tree-clad shore.

It was here, in the early part of the seventeenth century, that Sir George Hay, afterwards High Chancellor of Scotland, built an iron-works and staffed it with English labourers. A minister was required who could preach well in English, and the Rev. Farquhar MacRae of Kintail was chosen for the position. He and Sir George Hay became very friendly—so much so that, when Sir George left, he had persuaded " Mr. Farquhar " to go with him to London.

But Roderick Mackenzie and the young laird, Colin of Kintail, intervened and secured the services of this well-loved minister for the parish of Kintail.

The Laird of Gairloch at this time was John Roy Mackenzie, grandson of the celebrated Hector Roy who was instrumental in securing the lands of Gairloch for the MacKenzies. The story of the Clan battles for these lands is typical of Highland history during the days of the feuds.

In 1480, Gairloch was held by the MacLeods, and the Laird, Allan MacLeod, was married to the daughter of Alexander the Just, Baron of Kintail. Allan, however, was assassinated by his own two brothers, who secretly nursed a fierce hatred of the house of Kintail. With him were slain his two young sons. The distracted wife returned to Kintail, where her brother, Hector Roy, took up her cause, obtaining a commission from the King for the destruction of the MacLeods of

BEN KILLILAN AND SLOPES OF GLEN ELCHAIG FROM THE SOUTH

Gairloch. A member of the Clan MacRae, as usual supporting the MacKenzies, met the two murderers of Allan MacLeod and slew them single-handed. In 1494, Hector Roy received a Crown charter for the lands of Gairloch, but fierce fighting between the rival clans continued until the time of his grandson, John Roy, when the MacKenzies finally obtained the upper hand.

The country around lovely Loch Maree is also rich in tales of Bonnie Prince Charlie, for it was by way of Letterewe, Ardlair and north along the banks of Loch an Tolldoire that the fugitive Prince sent messengers to Poolewe to enquire for tidings of the French ship in which he was hoping to escape to the Continent.

At Slatadale, opposite the cluster of green islands and the brooding hills around Ben Lair, our road turned westward into the forest. Reaching Loch Bad na Sgalaig, we followed the foaming River Kerry between slopes carpeted with the soft mauve of the new heather.

Past the dark trees and the singing waters. Past the lane to Shieldaig —and, at last, over the brae to the great sweep of Loch Gairloch.

" Oh! " said my sister, " Look at the sands! "—and we sat there and looked to our heart's content, while the bus disgorged passengers at the big hotel.

After we had found lodgings at a white house in Strath, we went down on to the shore, took off our shoes, and paddled like children on the fringe of the incoming tide. Tiny drifts of pink and yellow cockle-shells added colour to the warm gold. The water was icy, and Jeannie obviously thought we were mad—until we started to run over the warm sand. Then, eyes alight and long coat flying, she joined in, became a puppy again for one delightful hour wherein we, too, reached out to touch hands with a forgotten childhood. . .

We spent three days in Gairloch. And each day we found some reason for wishing that it could be three years. We walked northward, past the Youth Hostel, to Big Sand, and spent a whole afternoon and evening looking for scallop-shells on the edge of the tide. Tired and happy, we came back to Mrs. MacLean's, and dropped into cosy beds, while the voice of the sea-wind crooned a hushing-song outside the window.

We walked to Loch Shieldaig. After lunch at the secluded hotel, we wandered along by the rocky shore (no sand here!) past the lichen-crusted rocks and rotting skeletons of old ships half-submerged in a green grave.

Brown islands all but blocked the entrance to the loch. About one of these, Fraoch Eilean (The Heather Island), an interesting story is told in the "old tales" of the district.

It is said that the MacLeods of Skye, having been told by a witch that they should retake Gairloch from the MacKenzies and MacRaes, set sail in their long black galley for the coveted land. They reached the bay, and fastened their boat to the Heather Island, between Shieldaig and Badachrò. But the Kintail men were ready. Two skilled archers, Dun Donald and Dun John, sons of Ian Liath, climbed a steep rock above the island. From here, they discharged their arrows, killing all the marooned MacLeods except two, who managed to regain the boat and escape. The rock on which the two brothers stood is now called Leac nan Saighead, or the Flat Stone of the Arrows.

Badachrò is a neat, white village, redolent of drying nets, old boats and the elusive tang of the sea. We were surprised to find a cleaning and dyeing establishment—small but well-advertised—in the single street.

From here, we looked across the great expanse of Loch Gairloch to Strath, and were able to pick out Mrs. MacLean's white house beyond the red roof of a byre. Seen from this angle, Strath looked big and scattered, a long line of crofts and cottages, running in a white curve round the bay. We could see the hotel and Church at Gairloch—but not a hint of those wonderful golden sands! Behind the green hillocks of the golf-course, the landscape dimmed to layer upon layer of dark forest, running back and up into the misty crags of the Flowerdale Hills.

The light mellowed. We turned slowly back through the woods, to tea at the hotel. Then, happy and sun-burned, we followed the shady road back to " home, supper and bed."

And the next day we went back to Kyle, with a golden memory of a golden land. A day then in Glen Shiel (when we were caught in torrents of rain)—and my sister's holiday was over.

Once more, Jeannie and I went to the station. My sister looked brown, happy and rested.

We parted with a smile. She to the chaotic but beloved newsreel office. I to my unfinished labour of love among the mountain fastnesses of Kintail.

CHAPTER XV

" SWAN LAKE " AND THE GHOSTS OF GLÒMACH

On the Sunday, I walked back to the Iron Lodge, Jeannie trotting excitedly at my heels. It was a fine, hazy day, and we covered the fifteen miles in good time. Mrs. Munro expressed surprise and delight at seeing us again so soon. Ostensibly, I had come to " relax "—but there yet remained one hill-loch to be seen, and I had hopes of getting some photographs of Glòmach, in spate after heavy rains.

The effusive greetings which passed between Jeannie and Snookie caused much mirth—especially when Morag came capering in and got mixed up in the general free-for-all. Bonkie, as usual, kept her distance, casting a cold yellow eye upon such antics from her perch on the window-sill.

We spent a lazy evening recovering from our tramp over rough gravel roads. The next day, I borrowed Mrs. Munro's cycle and set out in fine mist for Loch nan Ealachan, my last—and, from this angle, easiest—of the hill-lochs of Kintail.

Bouncing over the rough road, I pedalled leisurely along Glen Elchaig to the wooden bridge by the black telephone-kiosk. The atmosphere was close, with a suggestion of more rain. Leaving the cycle propped against some rocks, I struck up the good track running beside the hazel-bordered stream. It was already afternoon, and the midges danced and swarmed hungrily around me, sailing on waves of humid air. The burn sang softly over the brown stones. The heather tossed coral and magenta bells among wet bracken by the wayside. It was the big-belled, vivid variety; here it was as yet too early for the ling. Half-hidden in wet grass, the spotted orchis added splashes of pink and mauve to the quiet green. Cloud hovered over the nearer hills, and there was no sun. . . Further up the track, the bright bog-asphodel scattered the ground with gold spears.

The path remained good—firm and dry and well-defined—though, oddly enough, it was not marked on my map. By the stream, silver birches drooped delicately over tumbled grey stones. The pungent scent of bog-myrtle drifted errantly across the warm air.

I looked back into Glen Elchaig, a striking contrast at this point to the wild, bare country at the head of the glen. The bracken and heather moved lightly in the soft wind. Silver burns leapt down picturesque gorges thick with feathery trees. Yellow moths flitted across the fresh green grass, and sheep browsed placidly in the blue hollows of the hills. The path, climbing steadily now, was the best hill-track (and the driest) that I had yet encountered in my search for the elusive lochans hidden away in the Kintail hills.

Soon, the mist thickened; but the climb seemed neither long nor arduous, and there was no danger of my being lost in the cloud. For the first time, I saw the sundew in flower—tiny white bell-like blooms clustered on the top of a down-curving stem. The butterfly-orchis was poised daintily on her frail green stalk, swaying to the rhythm of the wind. All around waved great clusters of bell-heather, in places almost knee-high, with vivid bells of magnificent size.

Towards the summit, the path began to deteriorate a little; but it was still an improvement on other tracks I could mention! A fine rain was now drifting over the hills, imparting a dream-like, shadowy quality to their graceful curves and contours. All climbing was done with now, and I trudged along among low green hill-tops to the loch whose name had been a source of delight to me ever since I first found it on my map. The Loch of the Swans—or, as it was often called locally, Swan Lake. What a multitude of pictures it conjured up in the imagination! Indeed, a name chosen by some anonymous hill-poet—or perhaps by the " wee folk " themselves!

The path ran right on to the loch—and I was not disappointed. Lying among dark grey hills, calm, quiet and sheltered from the wind, Loch nan Ealachan might, indeed, have been a refuge for the wild swans after which it was named. It is a long, reedy stretch of grey-green water, with a group of islands huddled together in the centre, whereon, no doubt, the wild swans rested and hatched their downy cygnets out of reach of the wind and rain. I was surprised to find a small timber boat-house on the near shore—but was told afterwards that this loch is often visited by the local fishermen, and yields good trout. I saw only one tree—a slender rowan quivering on the far bank; and there was little colour in the landscape save for the patches of bright yellow moss adorning the tiny islands.

Loch nan Ealachan is the ideal goal for those who wish to visit a typical hill-loch without expending too much energy in the process. Cycling from the Iron Lodge, I attained the loch in just under two hours, after a short, pleasant and exhilarating climb over firm, dry ground. It can be found without a map, and is well worth a visit. My only regret was that conditions were too misty to allow me a photograph.

I began the descent.

The mist thickened as night approached; and, before I reached the Iron Lodge, it was raining heavily. All that night, the downpour continued—and, for once, I was not sorry, for it meant that I stood a chance of getting a fine picture of the Falls of Glòmach if the sun would shine long enough for me to take it!

Sure enough, the morning dawned bright and golden, with big white clouds drifting across a soft blue sky. The burns roared and foamed down the sodden hillsides, and I lost no time in cycling down to Carnach.

The route over the stepping-stones was now impassable, the stones themselves under two feet of water. But the two bridges at Carnach made light of the turbulent yellow streams, and I was soon tramping steadily up the track to the left of the lacy waterfall, about which there is a charming story:

In 1921, a ghillie to Mr. Wills of Killilan was one day wandering alone along the path beside this fall. Suddenly, to his great astonishment, he heard music coming from the stream—fine classical music such as he had heard broadcast from the Edinburgh and Glasgow concert halls. Full of wonder, he hastened back to tell his friends— but, though several people visited the fall at different times, the strange music was not heard again. It was suggested by a doctor on holiday that the lodestone in the burn might possibly have picked up wireless-waves from the air—but that was the nearest anyone could come to giving an explanation. Apart, that is, from the inhabitants of the glen, who had many explanations of their own. . .

Once on the top of the brae, I found myself tramping over a green, waterlogged plateau bounded by a semi-circle of cloud-capped hills. To my left lay Sgùrr na h-Eige and the sharp peak of Creag Ghlas. On my right, Meall Scouman rose proudly into a patch of clear sky. Crossing a hectic burn, I came to Loch a' Mhurachaidh, seen often from a distance, an irregular, sun-spangled pool bounded by a fringe of light reeds. Clouds travelled quietly in the grey waters, and the one tiny island with its bushy tree cast a green shadow among the weed.

I followed the well-defined path along the western shore. At the edge, the water was deep amber, with a hint of golden sand underneath. At the far end, a tiny thread of a burn ran out and along to another lochan, smaller, but infinitely more picturesque with its rugged little island bearing one naked tree and variety of water-plants thrusting green spears among the broken reeds.

Beyond this tiny sunlit pool, I looked up Coire Lochan towards the dark curve of Sgùrr nan Ceathreamhnan. The peaks of Stùc Beag and Stùc Mór were in heavy cloud, but I could distinguish the Allt a' Choire Lochan as it rushed down the dark hillside to join the foaming

THE PEAKS OF KINTAIL FROM MÀM RATTACHAN

Amhainn Gaorsaic below the string of lochs in the "bealach" to Glen Affric.

Soon, I reached the cairn whereon a rough arrow had been scratched to indicate the right track for the Falls of Glòmach. I splashed along the wet path and over the rise, from the summit of which I looked down at the frothing Amhainn Gaorsaic, surging along a green cleft in the hills . . . and softly, evilly, came to my ears again the muted thunder of falling waters.

From this angle, the entire landscape was dominated by the dark pinnacle of Càrnan Cruineachd, with its wet rocks shining in the fitful sun. Crossing the Glòmach burn was out of the question—the very sight of its surging current suggested the River of Death. I therefore ploughed along the north shore, over wet grass and peat, until I reached the dread point where the waters fall away into thundering immensity. Then, holding my breath, I crawled to the edge and looked once more over the chasm.

Clouds of white vapour flew up out of the black gorge, lashing my face and blinding my eyes. Far, far below, through a mist of spindrift, I could half-glimpse a green chasm winding away towards Glen Elchaig, with the fierce, foaming burn flowing into peat-black pools. The angry voice of the waters echoed and re-echoed from the walls of the great, rocky horse-shoe banking the fall.

Stunned by the noise and soaked by the flying spray, I at last drew back, found my camera, and began to scramble along the steep face of Meall Scouman to my right. Higher I went, and higher, pulling myself up by rocks and heather-roots. At last, on the top of a wet rock-face, I reached a point from which it was possible to photograph the fall. At exactly that moment, two young women came down the track from Dorusduain and peered cautiously over the chasm. I managed to get them in the picture—but, for some reason, the finished result was not the success I had hoped; probably because I was using old film.

Going back to the Iron Lodge, my shoes literally fell to pieces on my feet. To the great amusement of Mrs. Munro, I arrived with the soaked soles gaping away from the uppers, and nails sticking out in all directions. If I had not had the cycle waiting for me at Carnach, I might never have arrived at all!

After supper, I said goodbye to the long-suffering shoes, which were then burnt, with due solemnity, on the kitchen range!

I would repeat that this third route is the easiest way to the Falls of Glòmach, although the path from Carnach is not marked on most maps. It is well-known, however, among the shepherds and natives of Glen Elchaig, and, like the Dorusduain route, enables the visitor to see the Falls in spate. With a cycle, the path can be reached from Dornie in approximately two-and-a-half hours—or less, with a following wind. From Carnach, it takes just over an hour to walk to the Falls. This is an improvement on the perils of the Loch na Leitreach route over the stepping-stones, and the arduous tramp via Dorusduain.

For the student of history and legend, the whole district around the Falls of Glòmach is rich in lore and tradition. Following the Killilan road from Dornie (or, more properly, Ardelve), the wanderer looks across the narrowing neck of Loch Long to a great scooped-out bowl of rock in the flank of Beinn a' Mheadhoin, where it is said that a giant once sat down to fish in the dark waters. Above Sallachy foams a hill-burn reputed to be the bathing-place of a " Blue Lady," seen periodically by the shepherds as they climb the hillside in the early morning. Near the Smithy of Loch Long is another burn in which a " washer-wife " is rumoured to come out and wash shrouds in the phosphorescent water, attended by a little light resembling a will-o'-the-wisp. There is also the Allt Càisechan—the Burn of the Cheese—foaming down through a dark cleft called the Ciste Dhubh, or Black Box. There is a story of how a man once tried to hide in this cleft from the Army—and soon came out again, saying that he would rather face the guns! Legend has it that a fairy used to come out hereabouts and make cheese and dance in the moonlight; and the old people still relate how this story used to be told to children, to stop them going up on to the hill for blaeberries with which to black their faces.

About the Falls of Glòmach, the stories are legion. In addition to those I have recounted already, I heard, from a member of the Clan MacRae, the hair-raising tale of a shepherd from Lienassie, who once saw a woman standing on the brink of the Falls. Thinking it was the old woman who used to keep goats in the hills, he went away—but, presently, a strange feeling came over him, and he went back again, reluctantly, to the Fall. The woman was still standing there—and he needed no second glance to tell him that she was a visitant from the other world! Trembling, he came close in answer to her beckoning; and she gave him a message to take to some friends at Plockton. When he arrived at the house to which she had sent him, he found that his description of her exactly fitted that of a woman of that household who had recently committed suicide. The whole affair so upset the poor man's mind that he finally left the country, on the advice of friends, to " get the sea between himself and the ghost."

Another (less gruesome) tale recounts how a man from Duilich, visiting the Falls, saw a crowd of strangely-attired people gathered on the grass at the foot of the cataract. When he scrambled down the hillside to greet them, they all disappeared, leaving a woman in child-birth lying under a plaid. On questioning the woman, the man was told that he had arrived in the nick of time, as she was being stolen away by the fairies. Out of sympathy, he took her to his own house at Duilich, where she seems to have lived in comfort, with no questions asked, for about a year. Then, one day, the man went to Garve market, wearing the plaid which had been covering the woman when he found her by the Fall. Here, a stranger accosted him, recognised the plaid, and demanded the return of his wife, who had disappeared in childbirth a year ago! Unfortunately, legend does not record how this odd triangle was sorted out.

Duilich, the house where this woman is supposed to have spent the year following her rescue, is the house below the Iron Lodge—though the present up-to-date residence is, I think, a new one, built on the old site. I had the good fortune, while staying with Mrs. Munro, to meet the shepherds, both from Duilich and Carnach, who evinced great amusement at my interest in the " old tales " and supplied me with some valuable information during my search for the hill-lochs. It was from these gentlemen that I learned the name of Loch a' Mhurachaidh, which was not given on my map.

One of the most interesting features of my second visit to the Iron Lodge was the daily training of the baby collie, Morag, at which I was an enthralled spectator. " Leggy " now, her plump contours smoothing away into the graceful lines of a hill-dog, the puppy seemed to ooze energy, vitality and sheer mischief at every pore. Only, each evening, in the hands of her patient master, she became quiet, docile and obedient, though tense with excitement at the enthralling business of absorbing knowledge.

" Creep now, Morag! Creep now! " Hugh Munro would say, always in the same tone of voice; and, try as she might to ignore the command, the voice always won in the end. Down she would drop on her " tummy," eyes bright, ears pricked; and, slowly, slowly, she would begin to edge across the floor, on the trail of invisible sheep. Sometimes, she forgot, and stuck her hindquarters up in the air, or splayed her legs out like a giddy colt—but always the voice was there, gentle and compelling, coaxing her on to further effort. She was barely four months old—and yet, during the week I was there, she learned to creep on her own from one side of the kitchen to the other, intent only upon her master's voice and the business in hand. She learned to drop noiselessly at a word, and sit as still as a little dog carved in stone; and all the time her eyes never left her master's face and her soft ears quivered at a change in his voice. She certainly had the makings of a fine sheep-dog; and I have no doubt that, by this time, she has fully repaid the effort and patience expended on her training. (I wonder, sometimes, if the same thing could be done with a Skye terrier; but I fear Jeannie has too great a sense of humour to take the experiment seriously!)

To digress for a moment: speaking of sheep-dogs and sheep reminded me of the story of the "Pet Lamb of Kintail," a celebrated tale of this district, which was broadcast, learned in 1946. For the benefit of those who do not know the story, here it is, as told to me by one of the sons of the principal actor:

In the early 1880's, young Murdoch MacRae of Kintail had a sheep, which died, leaving a young lamb. This lamb he took home as a pet for the children, and it became very tame, roaming around loose in the garden and precincts of his home. Now, the estate at this time was rented by a wealthy American, Mr. W. L. Winans; and was given over to deer-forest. The gamekeeper, Mr. Ross, complained of the presence of this pet lamb, quoting the law, which forbade sheep on land reserved for deer. Murdoch MacRae, the father, defied him, and was summoned to Dingwall, where he lost the case. The MacRaes were not wealthy, and could afford to take matters no further; but the "Pet Lamb Case" came to the ears of the Laird, Mackenzie, who was sufficiently incensed to take it to the Court of Session, Edinburgh. Here, Lord Young gave the verdict in Murdoch MacRae's favour, remarking that deer-forest should be fenced in if the tenant intended to keep other animals out. Later, Mackenzie bought the lamb from the MacRaes, and saw to it that Mr. Winans left on the expiry of his lease. The whole affair was hailed as a triumph for the crofter, and was celebrated in fiery verse by a poet of the century, George Colburn.

I can still see the twinkle in Mr. John MacRae's eye as he sat in the neat parlour of his cottage, looking every inch a man of the sea, regaling me with the story while his wife brought me home-made scones and a glass of milk topped with at least half-an-inch of cream.

It is a story which, I think, would be enjoyed at the Iron Lodge— and I must remember to tell it on my next visit.

CHAPTER XVI

FAREWELL, FAIR LAND!

THE long, golden days of August came and went, and the month drew slowly to a close. There was no doubt about it now—Autumn was approaching, the serene sadness of it whispering in the sough of the sea, the wind that blew across the blooming heather. Quietly, the mantled hills waited under a greying sky—wave upon wave of living purple, melting softly into the blue mists of far horizons. There were mornings, now, when a finger of frost lay upon the rusting grasses, or traced the filigree of cobwebs in the garden wall, to presage the silver stillness of deep snows. On such mornings, the hills of Kintail lay calmly under their patched cloaks, resigned to their fate through faith in the renewal of beauty.

And, at last, in a similar spirit of resignation tinged with hope, I accepted mine. Haphazardly at first, I began to gather together my few possessions at Nostie Cottage, make out labels, arrange for carriage, and generally prepare the way for the inevitable journey South. My work was all but finished; and I was more than grateful to the Mathesons that my tenancy of the cottage had been extended to allow of its completion; especially as, during the whole of my summer in Kintail, there had been no slightest easing of the housing difficulty.

Jeannie did not take at all kindly to the remembered confusions of packing. Only too well did the poor little creature understand whereto it was leading! 'Buses, boats, trains, crowds—the whole terrifying paraphernalia attending a long journey. I tried to explain to her that next year we would have a caravan—but she was neither convinced nor reassured.

(I did not tell her until the last minute about the approaching trip to Stornoway. Somehow, I did not think she would share my views as to the necessity of including a visit to the Isle of Lewis in a book on Kintail!)

It was a morning of pale sunlight and drifting clouds when we said our last goodbye to Nostie Cottage. The melancholy bleat of the grown lambs followed us as we went out to the furniture-van. Behind us, the little grey house stood desolate and lonely in its overgrown garden, the sunlight glinting on the uncurtained windows and silvering the padlock on the front door. Mr. Matheson's horse clumped forlornly down the hillside and hung his head over the gate to the byre. Down the road, the blue hills behind Dornie were dark with moving shadows, brightening to purple and rose where a shaft of gold light touched the blooming heather. Beyond the near green hump of Avernish, Loch Alsh danced and glinted as if lit by a million silver fires. Sadly, I said goodbye to Mrs. Ingram and Miss Graham.

The big van carrying us and our belongings lurched and bumped along the winding road. Past Auchtertyre, the haunted road to Strome Ferry, Kirkton, Reraig and into the white curve which was the beginning of Balmacara Bay. I waved a grateful farewell to the little grocer's shop whose proprietor had lent me books and introduced me to Mr. Duncan MacRae of Balmacara, raconteur of many tales of the " Second Sight." Up Coille Mhór then, where the red crags rose proudly into a pale-blue sky, and I could still glimpse the stately home of the late Lady Hamilton, gleaming through the dark trees bordering the Bay. This gracious white house, together with the 8,000 acre estate of Balmacara, was bequeathed to the National Trust for Scotland, on its owner's death, during the period of our sojourn in Kintail.

The browning water-lilies danced a farewell saraband as we passed Lochan Iain Òig, and blowing whins lighted the slopes of the brae down to Kyle. After arranging with the station authorities about the transport of our furniture and larger luggage, we went to the hotel and began to lay plans for our final trip—the journey to Lewis, an island closely linked at one period of its history with the Lairds of Kintail.

On the Monday, after a quiet week-end, we met Mrs. Matheson off the 'bus from Dornie and proceeded down to the pier, loaded with raincoats, cameras, binoculars and a large supply of food. Jeannie was sulking again, and refused to take any interest in the adventure— but we would not let such a lack of enthusiasm damp our spirits. The *Loch Ness* did not sail until around three o'clock, so we had ample time to arrange our belongings and secure good seats out of the wind. The air was cold; and, while we watched, mist drifted over the Cuillin and cast a grey veil down on to the waters of the Sound. Even as we drew away from the pier, it began to rain. But still, away beyond the white port of Kyle of Lochalsh, the hills of Kintail were clear against a pale sky, Sgùrr Fhuaran dominating the entire range, lifting her proud head above her Sisters as if to catch a last glimpse of our little ship disappearing into the enchanted channels of the Isles.

It was raining heavily as we passed Scalpay, and the lower slopes of the Cuillin loomed darkly through heavy cloud. Mist hung low over the water to the west, and cloud rested on the flat top of Beinn na Leac on Raasay.

The sea was calm, however, and the boat throbbed steadily on her way north-west, while her passengers sat about in little groups, sheltering from the driving rain.

We reached Applecross in an hour, and crowded along the wet rail to look across grey water to a long row of grey-roofed houses sheltered by low, tree-clad hills. A small motor-launch put out from the pier to take off passengers, and bobbed away again over the calm water while our own engines chugged once more into life. An odour of cooking was now drifting up from the galley, and flocks of grey and black-backed gulls followed the *Loch Ness* as she drew away from the shallow waters of the little bay.

We steamed on up the Inner Sound, steadily northward now, a grey blur on each side marking the mainland and the east coast of Raasay. A bell rang from below, and we went down to refresh ourselves with finnan haddie and hot, strong tea—an indulgence for which we were to suffer later. After tea, we leaned over the port rail to look at the Island of Rona, with its white lighthouse and grey rock capped with blooming heather. The mist had lifted a little, and the flat-topped hills and cliffs of Trotternish lying beyond were dark blue against a watery sky. To starboard, patched now with faint sunlight, lay the hills of Shieldaig and Loch Torridon, a shadowy cluster of peaks and crags slashed by the shining curve of ebony-dark waters. Soon, these, too, were left astern, and we were steaming past Loch Gairloch and the familiar curve of golden sand in Strath Bay. Sunlight fell in quivering shafts on to the quiet waters, but the southern end of the bay remained dark, overshadowed by the cloud-capped hills of Flowerdale.

A porpoise rose and rolled quite near to the ship. We crossed the throbbing deck to the port side and looked away to the grotesque silhouette of the Storr Rock on Skye and the fantastic islands off the northern peninsula. Dimly, through the soft veils of mist, loomed the far coast of North Uist, blending and fading softly towards the faery-like outline of Harris and Lewis, changing and melting with the movement of the fingers of light travelling across the water. Stark against this misty background, the Shiant Islands thrust their weird heads out of the grey-gold sea, a distant cluster of dark specks huddling together on the lonely wastes of the Minch.

The wind freshened, and we huddled closer into our coats. Behind and to the east, the hills of Flowerdale faded into an undulating line of grey. We passed Rudha Réidh, with its lighthouse, and saw the

STORNOWAY¹ ISLE OF LEWIS, THE CASTLE, TOWN, AND HARBOUR

hills over Loch Broom and Ullapool, and the Summer Isles smudging the dark horizon with hazy blue, hardly distinguishable from the blue, strung-out clouds.

Skye and the Quirang faded sombrely into the quiet pattern of cloud and sea. But northward and westward the Midas touch of evening was transmuting the world to gold where long shafts of light fell trembling on to grey-green waters and spread a mist of moving gold over the dim outlines of the Outer Hebrides.

Two tireless gulls were still following us, veering and wheeling on the chill wind. Well out into the Minch now, the sturdy *Loch Ness* steamed on into the gathering evening, her red funnel belching smoke against the darkening sky. The rain had quite stopped, and we sailed tranquilly over smooth seas into a sunset of soft grey and softer gold. Jeannie slept, sprawled across my knees, while I sat scribbling idly, watching the long rolls of foam breaking from the prow and spreading along the sides of the ship, changing from white to palest turquoise before they merged again with the all-absorbing sea.

The sky over the Sutherland coast shaded to pale blue with an undertone of rose. Suddenly, sunlight flickered over shadowy distance, and the lovely landscape took on a tinge of coral. The Summer Isles were now but the faintest blue blur on the far horizon, but westward the Shiants stood out boldly, dark grey against the darkening hills of the Lewes.

The sun came right out then—a last gesture of magnificent defiance before she died. The whole of the western sea was now glittering and dancing in a million particles of living gold. The increasing wind whipped up clots of creamy foam on the crests of the smooth rollers, and the good ship lifted proudly to the swell.

We could now see the flat coastline of the Eye Peninsula, and the string of black, jagged rocks beyond the Shiant Islands, like a weird procession of sea-denizens or the coils of some vast amphibious creature living among the haunted isles. Northward, on the horizon, the

Stornoway herring-fleet went about its business in the sunset, sending up columns of black smoke into the quiet sky.

The gold deepened. The nearing coast of Lewis turned to a land of richest green and gold, with lime-coloured shadows in the hollows of the little hills. We could now see the clustered houses of Stornoway and the wireless pylons on the Eye Peninsula. A pathway of fire was running across the western sea, and the sky was patched with peacock-blue. The far hills of Sutherland lay astern, a line of palest lavender against a pale saffron sky.

It began to rain again, and a perfect rainbow hung in a great shining arch over the olive-green water. The colours changed and changed again over the Hebrides before the sun finally died behind the Outer Isles.

We came into Stornoway in the half-light of the autumn dusk. It was still bright enough to distinguish the colours of the buildings— red and green scattered lavishly among the more sombre grey, with a fine clock-tower and castle looming behind the low buildings along the wharf.

We drew in to the crowded pier, and went ashore. Already, the trawlers and drifters were in, and the nets stretched to dry along the harbour walls. Seagulls screamed and soared over the fish-barrels and settled in flocks on old boats lying at anchor off-shore. Sailors and fishermen in Shetland pull-overs trudged up and down the wharf or smoked contentedly, leaning against the sea-wall. One by one, the lights awoke in the town, and we went happily through the back-streets to our hotel. It was then nine-thirty, but we were straightway provided with an excellent fish-dinner and every possible attention. Afterwards, we were shown to our room—the walls of which, oddly enough, were lavishly decorated with cartoons of Disney's " Ferdinand the Bull " !

It was only there, in a quiet corner by the bedside, that poor Jeannie could be persuaded to eat.

179

I should have liked to spend a month in Lewis. There was so much to see, and the four days at our disposal were not sufficient to cover a tenth of the ground. We did, however, take the 'bus to Callernish to see the famous "false men"—and, although it poured with rain incessantly during the trip, we were able to see sufficient to obtain an impression of the landscape.

The 'bus was very old and rickety, but it sped gallantly along the winding roads, through the flat black land with its tinkers' camps and peat-heaps and great stretches of heathery waste running away to the grey sea. Everywhere we saw peat, stacked in neat piles by the wayside or heaped against the walls of the old stone cottages ready for use in the bleak days of winter. In the villages of Barvas and Bragor, we found traces of the old " black houses " with one chimney in the centre —but everywhere thatched cottages were being replaced by modern villas. The outstanding feature of this part of the island was its barrenness and the absence of trees.

Beyond Shawbost, the land became more uneven, and the road wound between grim, rocky hills dotted with sheep and hardy-looking cattle. The 'bus was now crowded, and jolted merrily on its way through Carloway, Dùn Carloway and Tolstacholis, where we could see across to the islands of Berndra, with a hint of Uig, supposed birthplace of the Brahan Seer, beyond.

At Callernish, we braved the driving rain to look at the " standing stones," rising weirdly on the top of their hillock, crusted with lichen. Unfortunately, weather conditions made a proper examination impossible, and we dashed down the hill again in teeming rain with only a hazy impression of this strange memorial to a forgotten age.

Back in Stornoway, we spent another day visiting a tweed-mill, where a most obliging guide showed us every stage in the process of weaving Harris tweed, from the dyeing and " teasing " of the great bales of sheepswool to the final clipping and stamping of the finished product. On the whole, it seemed a very fair arrangement between the mill-owners and the private crofter. Though a certain amount of chemical dyes are used—especially for the brighter colours—the bulk of the wool is dyed by the crofter himself, with natural dyes obtained from mosses, heather and peats. It is then blended, teased and spun up into yarn, which is sent back to the crofter for weaving up into tweed. On its second visit to the factory, it is washed, shrunk, trimmed and rolled up into great bales, each duly sprayed with water and anti-moth mixture. Cheviot-cross wool gives a soft finish, and black-faced wool a hard, hairy finish; and our guide was at pains to explain that the distinctive odour of Harris tweed is due to its being woven in an atmosphere of peat fires.

On the day of our departure, we spent the morning exploring the Castle, one-time home of Lord Leverhulme, from whom it passed to the Mathesons. It had been occupied by the "military" during the recent War, and the long, bare corridors were still adorned with signs pointing the way to air-raid shelters and dressing-stations. Outside —a vivid reminder of post-war chaos—a company of "squatters" were encamped in the huts formerly occupied by the Navy. The red-brick castle seemed to look down with dignity upon the array of perambulators and lines of washing, as if still a little bewildered by the "signs of the times." We were told that the Stornoway "squatters" were some of the pioneers of the movement—so no one could accuse the Isle of Lewis of being out-of-touch with the life of the big cities !

We walked through the large, bare rooms with their embossed ceilings and elaborately-carved mantelpieces. The castle was in the process of redecoration, and smelled of plaster and new paint. We climbed a dark spiral staircase to the top of the tower, and looked down on to the whole of Stornoway, spread out like a variegated tapestry below, with its brightly-coloured buildings, low green hills, and the great blue sweep of the bay, dotted with islands, fishing-smacks, and slim white yachts resting like birds on the sunlit water. The caretaker of the castle pointed out to us a cairn on the arm of the bay, marking where Prince Charles spent a night; and from there our gaze was led round and inland, over houses, streets and church-towers, to the pylons on the Eye Peninsula, the clustered hangers of the airfield, and the modern mill and factory buildings on the north curve of the bay. Immediately below us, beyond the squatters' camp, the herring-fleet lay sheltering against the net-strewn harbour-wall, though activity on the scrubbed decks of the ships revealed their preparations for putting to sea again on the turn of the tide.

Certainly, I thought, the Isle of Lewis to-day was a very different place from the remote and wild stronghold which came into the possession of the Lord of Kintail in 1610. According to the old histories, there had been, at that time, no marriages or baptisms on the island for forty years ; and so concerned was the Lord Kenneth over the " wild ways " of the inhabitants that he took the Rev. Farquhar MacRae, a noted minister who later became Constable of Eilean Donan Castle, along with him to the island to bring Christianity to the people. It is recorded that the Rev. Farquhar entered into the task with characteristic zest, and baptised the Lewismen *en masse* with a besom broom dipped in holy water, which he sprinkled over crowds of all ages up to fifty. He then set about marrying couples who had lived together for years, and, before his return to Kintail, had become a figure of admiration and respect among his new " flock."

Descending from the tower of the castle, we then walked back through the picturesque grounds into the town. Here, wandering through the narrower streets at the back of the harbour, we came upon the little Church of St. Peter, an Anglican sanctuary built in 1839, having an ancient font and turret-bell. It was small, dark, ornate and very beautiful, redolent of old wood and chrysanthemums, with an exquisitely-carved Sixteenth Century altar. I was spiritually at home here, and could have spent the afternoon absorbing its atmosphere of peace—but we had yet much to do before our boat sailed.

We therefore returned to the hotel, and set once more about the laborious business of packing.

We left Stornoway in darkness and drizzling rain. As Jeannie and I walked down to the quay, a piper began to play softly from the doorway of one of the houses. Lamplight slanted on to wet pavements, and silver drops fell in showers from the housetops to join the thin streams pouring over the kerb into the swirling gutters. Dimly, against the harbour-wall, the lighted masts of the fishing-fleet swayed to the roll of the tide.

Mrs. Matheson was already aboard, having resisted the temptation of a last cup of tea at the hotel. We climbed the slippery gang-plank and joined the throng queueing for mattresses on the lower deck. As there were about a dozen to be divided among several hundred people, it is not surprising that we were unlucky!

Later, we went up into the bows and sat on a coil of wet rope, watching the lights of Stornoway fading astern and the distant beacons awaking on the Sutherland coast. There was no sound here but the soft throbbing of the engines, the sigh of the wind, and the hiss of water rolling away from the prow of the ship. Thus, well-wrapped up against the rain, and fortified by odd cups of tea from a friend's flask, we spent the night. . .

As I said, I would have liked to spend a month in Lewis. It has many historical and traditional connections with Kintail, and is, besides this, an island of great charm and friendliness, one of those delightful places where the inhabitants seem to go out of their way to make the stranger feel at home. During my brief visit, I met with nothing but kindliness, courtesy and the kind of co-operation which asks nothing in return. To me, the warmth and generosity of the people of " the Lewes " more than atones for the barrenness of the country.

Among the Prophecies of the Brahan Seer, there is one (now fulfilled) which touches upon the link between Lewis and Kintail. " The day will come," prophesied Coinneach Odhar, many years before this happened, " when the Lewismen shall go forth with their hosts to battle, but they will be turned back by the jawbone of an animal smaller than an ass."

During the troubled days of the '45, a company of Jacobites was raised in Lewis and commanded by Captain Colin Mackenzie. This company set sail, in two ships, for the mainland, and entered the bay near Poolewe. Here (so the tale runs), they were espied by Lord Seaforth, who was just finishing a dinner of sheep's head. The appearance of these ships was not in line with his plans, and he turned them back by waving the sheep's jaw-bone at them and indicating that they should return at once to Lewis! This, they did, and thus the prophecy of the Brahan Seer was fulfilled.

Other predictions foretell the over-running of the Island by sheep and deer, and how much of the cultivated land would fall to waste between " Uig of the mountains and Ness of the plains." This last has come to pass during recent years.

Lewis is proud of her sons, and justly so. During my few days in Stornoway, I attended the cinema to see *I Know where I'm Going*, in which a Stornoway lad, Murdo Morrison, had a substantial part. The little theatre was crowded, and a thrill seemed to run through the audience when " Kenny Baker " came on to the screen. Though I was seeing this film for the third time, it seemed completely fresh— perhaps because I could not help seeing it from the angle of this particular audience, and sharing their pride in the " boy who had made good."

Back in Kyle of Lochalsh, I made one last excursion on the mainland before saying goodbye to the West Coast. Over a week-end, I explored the estate of Balmacara from Kyle to Duncraig and thence over by Lochan Iain Òig down to Balmacara and Kirkton. I visited Duirinish with its ancient trees, and looked out (through teeming rain) across Plockton and lovely Loch Carron to the high hills. I found Loch Lundie, with its waving larches, and saw the sun set from the top of Coille Mhór, turning " Young John's Lochan " to a sheet of fire.

Best of all, I climbed the hill behind Auchtertyre, and gazed through the blue folds of dusk to the Five Sisters of Kintail.

Below me, in the deep green hollow, I could see Nostie Cottage—my home for six months—with its red byre and the wild garden where I had sun-bathed and scribbled through the long days of an unforgettable summer. And there, all around, were the houses of my friends and neighbours—the Post Office, the cottages and little farms, with the silver gleam of Loch Alsh beyond. Along the straight road towards Ardelve, a flock of overgrown lambs jostled sleepily, the wakeful collies ever at their heels. Over flat-topped Beinn a' Mheadhoin, rosy clouds hung motionless in space, casting dark-blue shadows down the rugged flank of the hill.

My thoughts wandered down to the white town of Dornie, out of sight, but lovely, as always, in the dusk. There, in my mind's eye, was the bridge across Loch Long—the ferry to Totaig, the little Church of Scotland up the brae, and the Roman Catholic Church looking across the weed-strewn shores of the loch towards Conchra and the Free Church at Ardelve. There were the two hotels, " Dornie " and " Loch Duich," their gaily-lighted windows flickering a message to each other through the gathering shadows—and there, proud and aloof upon its island, the Castle of Eilean Donan watched over the junction of the three lochs, its grey stones afire with the light of the dying sun.

History, legend, tradition were everywhere, and snatches of the old stories came and went like the moving shadows. There was the tale of the old woman who lived in a castle at Totaig, Cruagach by name, who possessed an enormously long pair of tongs with which she used to stretch across Loch Alsh to steal the peats from Ardelve first thing in the morning! There was the giant who threw a boulder at one of the escaping clansmen—the great rock now lying just off the Ardelve shore. Strangest—and most amusing—of all, was the story of the two lairds who each wagered that his servant could swim further than the other, and all went down to the shore to prove it. One of the servants could not swim at all—but, on the instructions of his laird, he arrived with a huge skin of food strapped on to his shoulders, explaining that he must take provisions for the long journey. This so discouraged the other servant that he refused the contest altogether, thus losing his laird the wager!

From Dornie, I wandered on in spirit through Inverinate, Morvich, and so down to the Kintail Lodge and the beginnings of Glen Shiel. It was not hard to conjure up pictures here, for I could actually see the Five Sisters rising above the head of Loch Duich—and, anew, I thrilled to the beauty of them—marvelled at their purity of line—followed, with hungry eyes, their clefts and gorges to the cloud-capped summits which I felt would be etched on my memory for evermore.

The hand of Progress is now upon Kintail, with the recent arrival of the Hydro-Electric scheme. The changes will be welcome, bringing added comfort to the Highland homes. But the Five Sisters, under the National Trust, will remain aloof and wild and ever beautiful.

Was it my imagination—or did they really stretch out the shadowy arms of their mists in the dusk, beckoning me back for another year. . ?